STUDENT SOLUTIONS MANUAL FOR USE WITH

Fundamental Accounting Principles

VOLUME 2

TENTH CANADIAN EDITION
CHAPTERS 12–20

KERMIT D. LARSON
University of Texas at Austin, Emeritus

TILLY JENSEN
Northern Alberta Institute of Technology

RAY CARROLL
Dalhousie University

Prepared by
Tilly Jensen
Northern Alberta Institute of Technology

McGraw-Hill Ryerson

Toronto Montréal Boston Burr Ridge, IL Dubuque, IA Madison, WI New York San Francisco
St. Louis Bangkok Bogotá Caracas Kuala Lumpur Lisbon London Madrid
Mexico City Milan New Delhi Santiago Seoul Singapore Sydney Taipei

McGraw-Hill
Ryerson Limited

A Subsidiary of The McGraw·Hill Companies

STUDENT SOLUTIONS MANUAL
for use with
Fundamental Accounting Principles, Volume Two
Tenth Canadian Edition

ISBN: 0-07-090515-0

1 2 3 4 5 6 7 8 9 10 CP 0 9 8 7 6 5 4 3 2

Printed and bound in Canada

Vice President and Editorial Director: Pat Ferrier
Senior Sponsoring Editor: Nicole Lukach
Developmental Editor: Katherine Goodes
Supervising Editor: Carrie Withers
Senior Marketing Manager: Jeff MacLean
Production Coordinator: Madeleine Harrington
Printer: Canadian Printco

Contents

Chapter 12   Capital Assets

EXERCISES

Exercise 12-1 (10 minutes)

Invoice cost...	$11,500
Freight costs..	260
Steel mounting	795
Assembly	375
Raw materials for testing	30
Less: discount ($11,500 × 2%).....................	230
Total acquisition costs	$12,730

Exercise 12-3 (15 minutes)

Cost of land:

Purchase price for land	$225,000
Purchase price for old building	120,000
Demolition costs for old building...	34,500
Landscaping	51,000
Total cost of land..	$430,500

Cost of new building:

Construction costs...	$1,440,000
Less cost of land improvements	85,500
Cost of new building..	$1,354,500

Journal entry:

Land..	430,500	
Land Improvements	85,500	
Building...	1,354,500	
Cash...		1,870,500
To record costs of plant assets.		

Exercise 12-5 (15 minutes)

Year   Rate/unit = (42,300 − 6,000)/181,500 = $0.20
2001...................... $.20 × 38,300 = 7,660
2002...................... $.20 × 41,150 = 8,230
2003...................... $.20 × 52,600 = 10,520
2004...................... $.20 × 49,450 = 9,890

Exercise 12-7 (30 minutes)

Year	Straight-line Method		Double-Declining Balance Method	
	Amortization Expense[1]	Book Value at December 31	Amortization Expense[2]	Book Value at December 31
2001	$29,250	$117,750	$73,500	$73,500
2002	29,250	88,500	36,750	36,750
2003	29,250	59,250	6,750	30,000
2004	29,250	30,000	0	30,000

1. (147,000 − 30,000)/4 = 29,250 each year
2. 2001: 50% × 147,000 = 73,500
   2002: 50% × (147,000 − 73,500) = 36,750
   2003: 117,000* − 110,250** = 6,750

* Maximum allowable accumulated amortization; 147,000 − 30,000
**Accumulated amortization to date = 73,500 + 36,750

Fundamental Accounting Principles, Tenth Canadian Edition

Exercise 12-9 (20 minutes)

a.

	Cost Information						Amortization		
Description	Date of Purchase	Amortization Method	Cost	Salvage	Life	Balance of Accum. Amort. Dec. 31, 2000	Amortization Expense for 2001	Balance of Accum. Amort. Dec. 31, 2001	
Building	2 May 1995	S/L	$325,000	$125,000	10 yr.	$113,333	$20,000[1]	$133,333[2]	
Land	2 May 1995	N/A	120,000	N/A	N/A	0	0	0	
Truck	25 Jan 1998	DDB	40,000	5,000	6 yr.	27,654	4,115[3]	31,769[4]	

1. $(325,000 - 125,000)/10 = 20,000/\text{year}$
2. $113,333 + 20,000 = 133,333$
3. Rate = $2/6 = .3333$ or 33.33%
   $33.33\% \times (40,000 - 27,654) = 4,115$
4. $27,654 + 4,115 = 31,769$

b. Amortization has not been calculated on the land because land does not amortize.

Exercise 12-11 (15 minutes)
a.

	Year 1	Year 2	Year 3	Year 4	Year 5
Income before amortization	$57,000	$57,000	$57,000	$57,000	$57,000
Amortization expense[1]	24,360	24,360	24,360	24,360	24,360
Net income	$32,640	$32,640	$32,640	$32,640	$32,640

b.

	Year 1	Year 2	Year 3	Year 4	Year 5
Income before amortization	$57,000	$57,000	$57,000	$57,000	$57,000
Amortization expense[2]	62,720	37,632	21,448	0	0
Net income (loss).............................	$(5,720)	$19,368	$35,552	$57,000	$57,000

1. $(156,800 - 35,000)/5 = 24,360$
2. Rate = $2/5 = .40$ or 40%
   Year 1: $156,800 \times 40\% = 62,720$
   Year 2: $(156,800 - 62,720) \times 40\% = 37,632$
   Year 3: $[(156,800 - 35,000) - (62,720 + 37,632)] = 21,448$

Exercise 12-13 (15 minutes)

Rate = $(53,000 - 6,800)/2,310,000 = \$0.02/\text{unit}$

Year	Units-of-production Amortization
2001	15,000 $750,000 \times .02 = 15,000$
2002	15,800 $790,000 \times .02 = 15,800$
2003	15,400* $801,000 \times .02 = 1\cancel{6,020}$
Total	46,200

*Recall that maximum accumulated amortization is:
 = Cost – Salvage
 = $53,000 – $6,800 = $46,200.
Therefore, the maximum amortization expense that can be taken in 2003 is $15,400 [$46,200 – ($15,000 + $15,800)].

Fundamental Accounting Principles, Tenth Canadian Edition

Exercise 12-15 (25 minutes)

Year	Straight-Line	Amortization Double-Declining-Balance	Units-of-Production (same as Exercise 12-13*)
2001	(53,000 − 6,800)/3 = 15,400 × 6/12 = 7,700	Rate = 2/3 = .67 or 67% 53,000 × 67% × 6/12 = 17,755	15,000
2002	15,400	(53,000 − 17,755) × 67% = 23,614	15,800
2003	15,400	(53,000 − 6,800) − (17,755 + 23,614) = 4,831	15,400
2004	15,400 × 6/12 = 7,700	0	0

*Units-of-production is a usage-based method therefore partial periods do not impact the calculations as they do for both the straight-line and double-declining-balance methods which are time-based.

Exercise 12-17 (10 minutes)

a. $(21{,}750 - 2{,}250)/4 = 4{,}875/\text{year} \times 2 \text{ years} = 9{,}750 \text{ amortization}$
Book value $= 21{,}750 - 9{,}750 = 12{,}000$

b. $[(21{,}750 - 9{,}750) - 1{,}800]/3 = 3{,}400$

Exercise 12-19 (15 minutes)

a.

2005			
Mar. 27	Equipment..	28,000	
	Cash..		28,000
	To record installation of new motor.		

b.

2005			
Dec. 31	Amortization Expense, Equipment............................	12,171	
	Accumulated Amortization, Equipment.................		12,171
	To record revised amortization for 2005.		

Calculations:

Revised
amortization = $\dfrac{(107{,}000 + 28{,}000 - 64{,}500^*) - 15{,}000}{7 - 3\ 7/12^{**} = 3.42 \text{ years remaining}} \times 9/12 = 12{,}171$
for 2005

* Accumulated Amortization, Equipment

	6,000	2001	⟵——— (4/12)
	18,000	2002	⟵——— (12/12)
	18,000	2003	⟵——— (12/12)
	18,000	2004	⟵——— (12/12)
	4,500	To Mar. 27/05	⟵——— (9/12)
		Balance at	
	64,500	March 27, 2005	**(3 7/12)

Fundamental Accounting Principles, Tenth Canadian Edition

Exercise 12-21 (20 minutes)

a.	Accumulated Amortization, Van..	21,850	
	Cash..	16,650	
	Van...		38,500
b.	Accumulated Amortization, Van..	21,850	
	Cash..	18,400	
	Van...		38,500
	Gain on Disposal...		1,750
c.	Accumulated Amortization, Van..	21,850	
	Cash..	13,000	
	Loss on Disposal...	3,650	
	Van...		38,500

Exercise 12-23 (10 minutes)

1. 190,000 – 105,000 = 85,000 book value

2. Book value of the assets given up = (85,000 + 164,000)= 249,000
   Less: Assets received... = 220,000
   Loss on exchange 29,000

3. 220,000

Exercise 12-25 (10 minutes)

2001			
Dec. 31	Amortization Expense, Mineral Deposit....................	398,310	
	Accumulated Amortization, Mineral Deposit		398,310
	3,633,750/1,425,000 = 2.55/tonne		
	2.55 × 156,200 tonnes = 398,310		
31	Amortization Expense, Machinery	18,744	
	Accumulated Amortization, Machinery		18,744
	171,000/1,425,000 = 0.12/tonne		
	0.12 × 156,200 tonnes = 18,744		

Exercise 12-27 (10 minutes)

a.

2002

Jan. 1	Current assets..	236,000	
	Land	294,000	
	Building..	69,000	
	Equipment	42,000	
	Goodwill...	211,500	
	Liabilities		132,500
	Cash		100,000
	Notes Payable		620,000
	To record the purchase of net identifiable assets and goodwill.		

b.

2002

Dec. 31	Amortization Expense, Goodwill.....................................	14,100	
	Goodwill...		14,100
	To record amortization of goodwill; 211,500/15 = 14,100.		

Exercise 12-29 (10 minutes)

Land (new)...	120,000	
Loss on disposal*..	13,000	
Land (old)		130,000
Cash...		3,000
To record exchange of assets.		

*This is an exchange involving nonmonetary assets because cash is less than 10% of the consideration (book value of asset given up + cash paid = 130,000 + 3,000 = 133,000) therefore the new land is to be recorded at $133,000, the consideration given. However, because the consideration given is greater than the market value of the land received, a loss must be recorded. The loss is equal to the difference between the consideration given and the market value of the asset received.

PROBLEMS

Problem 12-1B (25 minutes)

Part 1

	Land	Building B	Building C	Land Imprmnts. B	Land Imprmnts. C
Purchase price*	$ 769,500	$459,000		$121,500	
Demolition...................	117,000				
Landscaping	172,500				
New building			$1,356,000		
New improvements					$101,250
Totals...........................	$1,059,000	$459,000	$1,356,000	$121,500	$101,250

*Allocation of purchase price:

	Appraised Value	Percent of Total	Apportioned Cost
Land..	$ 792,585	57%	$ 769,500
Building B	472,770	34	459,000
Land Improvements B	125,145	9	121,500
Totals.......................................	$1,390,500	100 %	$1,350,000

Part 2

June 1	Land	1,059,000	
	Building B...	459,000	
	Building C...	1,356,000	
	Land Improvements B...	121,500	
	Land Improvements C...	101,250	
	Cash		3,096,750
	To record costs of plant assets.		

Problem 12-3B (30 minutes)

Amortization Method:

Year	Straight-line	Double-declining balance	Units-of-production
2001	(145,000 − 25,000)/5 = 24,000/year × 6/12 = 12,000	Rate = 2/5 = .40 or 40% 145,000 × 40% × 6/12 = 29,000	Rate = (145,000 − 25,000)/100,000 = 1.20/km 1.20 × 5,800 = 6,960
2002	24,000	(145,000 − 29,000) × 40% = 46,400	1.20 × 19,400 = 23,280
2003	24,000	(145,000 − 29,000 − 46,400) × 40% = 27,840	1.20 × 22,850 = 27,420
2004	24,000	(145,000 − 29,000 − 46,400 − 27,840) × 40% = 16,704	1.20 × 25,700 = 30,840
2005	24,000	56*	1.20 × 19,980 = 23,976
2006	12,000	0	120,000 − 112,476** = 7,524**
Totals	120,000	120,000	120,000

* Maximum allowed = $56 [$120,000 − ($29,000 + $46,400 + $27,840 + $16,704)]
** Maximum allowed = $7,524 [$120,000 − ($6,960 + $23,280 + $27,420 + $30,840 + $23,976)]

Problem 12-5B (15 minutes)

a.

```
2002
Dec. 31   Amortization Expense, Van ..........................................    13,750
                 Accumulated Amortization, Van.........................                  13,750
                 To record annual amortization;
                 (125,000 – 15,000)/8 = 13,750

     31   Amortization Expense, Machinery ...........................    31,667
                 Accumulated Amortization,
                 Machinery ......................................................                  31,667
                 To record annual amortization;
                 Rate = 2/4 = .50 or 50%;
                 50% × (320,000 – 256,667) = 31,667
```

b.

ACE MECHANICAL
Partial Balance Sheet
December 31, 2002

Capital assets:
  Plant and equipment:

Delivery van	$125,000	
Less: Accumulated amortization	96,250	$28,750
Machinery	320,000	
Less: Accumulated amortization	288,334	31,666
Total plant and equipment		$60,416

Problem 12-7B (45 minutes)

Year	Straight-Line[a]	Units-of-Production[b]	Double-Declining-Balance[c]
2001	$ 22,360	$ 23,520	$ 52,000
2002	33,540	36,960	57,200
2003	33,540	33,600	34,320
2004	33,540	31,920	20,592
2005	33,540	26,600	3,588*
2006	11,180	15,100	0
Totals	$167,700	$167,700	$167,700

[a]Straight- line:

Cost per year = (195,000 – 27,300)/5 years = $33,540 per year × 8/12
= $22,360

Problem 12-7B *(continued)*

bUnits-of-production:
  Cost per unit = (195,000 – 27,300)/120,000 units = $1.40 per unit
                                                    (rounded)

Year	Units	Unit Cost	Amortization
2001	16,800	$1.40	$23,520
2002	26,400	1.40	36,960
2003	24,000	1.40	33,600
2004	22,800	1.40	31,920
2005	19,000	1.40	26,600
2006	22,100	1.40	15,100*
Total			$167,700

*Take only enough amortization in Year 2006 to reach the maximum
 accumulated amortization of $167,700.

cDouble-declining-balance:

  Rate = 2/5 = .40 or 40%
  2001: 40% × 195,000 × 8/12 = 52,000
  2002: 40% × (195,000 – 52,000) = 57,200
  2003: 40% × (195,000 – 52,000 – 57,200) = 34,320
  2004: 40% × (195,000 – 52,000 – 57,200 – 34,320) = 20,592
  2005: 167,700 – 164,112* = 3,588

  *Take only enough amortization in Year 2005 to reach the maximum
   accumulated amortization of $167,700.

Problem 12-9B (20 minutes)

2001

June 26	Truck	35,910	
	Cash		35,910
	To record purchase of new truck;		
	$34,200 + 1,710 sales tax.		
July 5	Truck	1,890	
	Cash		1,890
	To record installation of special racks.		
Dec. 31	Amortization Expense, Truck[1]	3,600	
	Accumulated Amortization, Truck		3,600
	To record amortization for half-year.		

2002

Mar. 15	Repair and Maintenance Expense	330	
	Cash		330
	To record repairs.		
Dec. 31	Amortization Expense, Truck[2]	5,300	
	Accumulated Amortization, Truck		5,300
	To record revised amortization		

1. $[(35,910 + 1,890) - 9,000]/4 \times 6/12 = \underline{3,600}$

2. $[(35,910 + 1,890) - 3,600 - 5,050]/(6 - .5 = 5.5) = \underline{5,300}$

Problem 12-11B (45 minutes)

(1)

2001

Jan. 9	Machine	68,400	
	Cash		68,400
	To record costs of loader.		
Jan. 10	Machine	14,400	
	Cash		14,400
	To record betterment and installation;		
	8,100 + 6,300 = 14,400.		

Problem 12-11B *(continued)*

(2)

Dec. 31	Amortization Expense, Machine...............................	24,000	
	Accumulated Amortization, Machine.....................		24,000

To record amortization;
[(68,400 + 14,400) – 10,800]/3 = 24,000.

2003
Mar. 29	Amortization Expense, Machine...............................	6,000	
	Accumulated Amortization, Machine.....................		6,000

To record amortization;
24,000 × 3/12 = 6,000.

(3a)

Mar. 29	Accumulated Amortization, Machine[1]......................	54,000	
	Cash..	35,250	
	Machine		82,800
	Gain on Disposal...		6,450

To record sale for cash of $35,250.

(3b)

Mar. 29	Accumulated Amortization, Machine........................	54,000	
	Cash..	24,150	
	Loss on Disposal..	4,650	
	Machine		82,800

To record sale for cash of $24,150.

(3c)

Mar. 29	Accumulated Amortization, Machine................	54,000	
	Cash..	22,050	
	Loss on Disposal	6,750	
	Machine...		82,800

To record insurance settlement.

1. 2001: 24,000
   2002: 24,000
   2003: 6,000
          54,000

Fundamental Accounting Principles, Tenth Canadian Edition

Problem 12-13B (60 minutes)

1.

2001

Jan.	1	Machine...	130,000	
		Cash..		130,000
		To record purchase of machine.		
	2	Machine...	3,390	
		Cash..		3,390
		To record capital repairs on machine.		
	2	Machine...	4,800	
		Cash..		4,800
		To record installation of machine.		

2.

Dec.	31	Amortization Expense, Machine...............................	17,170	
		Accumulated Amortization, Machine.....................		17,170
		To record amortization;		
		(138,190 – 18,000)/7 = 17,170		

2006

Apr.	1	Amortization Expense, Machine...............................	4,293	
		Accumulated Amortization, Machine.....................		4,293
		To record partial year's amortization;		
		17,170 × 3/12 = 4,293.		

3(a).

	30	Accumulated Amortization, Machine[1].........................	90,143	
		Cash..	30,000	
		Loss on Disposal[2]	18,047	
		Machine..		138,190
		Sold machine for $30,000.		

3(b).

	30	Accumulated Amortization, Machine.........................	90,143	
		Cash..	50,000	
		Machine..		138,190
		Gain on Disposal[3]		1,953
		Sold machine for $50,000.		

3(c).

	30	Accumulated Amortization, Machine.........................	90,143	
		Cash..	20,000	
		Loss on Disposal[4]	28,047	
		Machine..		138,190
		Received insurance settlement.		

Problem 12-13B *(continued)*

1. Accumulated amortization = $\overbrace{(17{,}170 \times 5 \text{ years})}^{\substack{\text{Amort. for 2001, 2002,} \\ \text{2003, 2004, and 2005.}}} + \overbrace{4{,}293}^{\substack{\text{Amort. for} \\ \text{2006.}}} = \underline{90{,}143}$

2. Gain (Loss) = Cash Proceeds − Book Value
   = 30,000 − (138,190 − 90,143) = <u>(18,047)</u>

3. Gain (Loss) = Cash Proceeds − Book Value
   = 50,000 − (138,190 − 90,143) = <u>1,953</u>

4. Gain (Loss) = Cash Proceeds − Book Value
   = 20,000 − (138,190 − 90,143) = <u>(28,047)</u>

Fundamental Accounting Principles, Tenth Canadian Edition

Problem 12-15B (45 minutes)

a. and c. Purchase and disposal of each machine.

1998

May 1   Machine 366-90.. 48,600

       Cash   48,600

       To record purchase of Machine 366-90.

2000

Aug. 5   Machine 366-91.. 36,000

       Accumulated Amortization, Machine 366-90[2] 24,300

             Machine 366-90..   48,600

             Cash   9,000

             Gain on Disposal...   2,700

       To record exchange of Machine 366-90.

2003

Feb. 1   Cash 9,000

       Accumulated Amortization, Machine 366-91[4] 25,560

       Loss on Disposal 1,440

             Machine 366-91..   36,000

       To record sale of Machine 366-91.

     1   Machine 367-11.. 53,100

             Cash   53,100

       To record purchase of Machine 367-11.

2004

Oct. 3   Cash 36,000

       Accumulated Amortization, Machine 367-11[6] 12,000

       Loss on Disposal 5,100

             Machine 367-11..   53,100

       To record sale of Machine 367-11.

b. Amortization expense on first December 31 of each machine's life

1998

Dec. 31   Amortization Expense, Machine 366-90[1] 7,200

             Accumulated Amortization, Machine 366-90   7,200

       To record amortization.

2000

Dec. 31   Amortization Expense, Machine 366-91[3] 6,000

             Accumulated Amortization, Machine 366-91   6,000

       To record amortization.

2003

Dec. 31   Amortization Expense, Machine 367-11[5] 4,800

             Accumulated Amortization,

             Machine 367-11..   4,800

       To record amortization.

Student Solutions Manual for Chapter 12

Problem 12-15B *(continued)*

1. $\dfrac{48,600 - 5,400}{4} = 10,800/\text{year} \times 8/12 = \underline{7,200}$

2. Amortization 1998:   7,200
                       1999:   10,800
                       2000:   6,300   (10,800 × 7/12)
   Accum. Amort   24,300

3. Rate = 2/5 = .40 or 40%
   40% × 36,000 × 5/12 = 6,000

4. 2000:   6,000
    2001: 40% × (36,000 − 6,000) =   12,000
    2002: 40% × (36,000 − 6,000 − 12,000) =   7,200
    2003: 40% × (36,000 − 6,000 − 12,000 − 7,200) × 1/12 =   360
                                                                   25,560

5. (53,100 − 5,400)/75,000 = $0.64/unit (rounded)

    2003: 7,500 units × 0.64/unit = 4,800

6. Amortization for Jan. 1/2004 to Oct. 3/2004:
   = 11,250 units × 0.64/unit =   7,200
                                             4,800
   Accum. Amort.   12,000

Fundamental Accounting Principles, Tenth Canadian Edition

Problem 12-17B (20 minutes)

(1)

2003				
June 25	Leasehold	75,000	
	Cash..		75,000
	To record payment for sublease.		

(2)

2004				
July 1	Rent Expense	28,000	
	Cash..		28,000
	To record annual lease rental.		

(3)

July 8	Leasehold Improvements..	90,950	
	Cash..		90,950
	To record costs of leasehold improv.		

(4)

Dec. 31	Rent Expense ($75,000/10 × 6/12)................................	3,750	
	Leasehold		3,750
	To record leasehold amortization.		

(5)

Dec. 31	Rent Expense ($90,950/10 × 6/12)................................	4,548	
	Leasehold Improvements.....................................		4,548
	To record leasehold improv. *amortization.*		

Chapter 13   Current Liabilities

EXERCISES

Exercise 13-1 (10 minutes)

a.	C	e.	L
b.	C	f.	L
c.	C	g.	C
d.	N	h.	C

Exercise 13-3 (15 minutes)

1.a.

2002			
Jan. 2	Land..	120,000	
	Notes Payable...		120,000
	To record issuance of 6%, 3-year note.		

1.b.

2002			
Dec.31	Notes Payable..	37,693	
	Interest Expense..	7,200	
	Cash..		44,893
	To record annual payment on note payable.		

2.

Liabilities:
Current liabilities:

Current portion of long-term note...	$39,955
Long-term note payable (less current portion of $39,955)	42,352

Exercise 13-5 (15 minutes)

2002
1. Nov. 30 Unearned Revenue.. 12,000
                 Service Revenue   12,000
             To record earned portion of unearned revenue;
             $48,000/6 = $8,000 × 1.5 = $12,000.

2.   30 Office Salaries Expense 2,500.00
           Sales Salaries Expense 1,800.00
                 Employees EI Payable*...............................   103.20
                 Employees' Income Taxes Payable.....................   1,290.00
                 Employees' CPP Payable*...............................   157.20
                 Payroll Payable...   2,749.60
             To record accrued payroll amounts.

3.   30 Utilities Expense 1,380
                 Accounts Payable   1,380
             To record accrued utilities for November.

           *Note: The employer's portion of EI Payable and
           CPP Payable were not provided and have, therefore,
           been ignored

Exercise 13-7 (20 minutes)

a.

Mar. 10 Machinery 60,000
               Cash   60,000
           Purchased machinery for cash.

b.

Mar. 10 Machinery 60,000
               Accounts Payable   60,000
           Purchased machinery on credit; terms 1/30, n60.

Apr. 9 Accounts Payable 60,000
               Cash   59,400
               Machinery   600
           Paid the account within the discount period;
           $60,000 × 1% = $600.

Exercise 13-7 (continued)

c.

Mar. 10	Machinery	60,000	
	Notes Payable		60,000
	Purchased machinery with a note.		

Mar. 10	Notes Payable	60,000	
	Interest Expense..	6,000	
	Cash		66,000
	Paid the note; $60,000 × 10% = $6,000.		

Exercise 13-9 (25 minutes)

1.

Days in December...	31
Minus date of note	1
Days remaining in December	30
Add days in January...	31
Add days in February	28
Days to equal 90 days or Maturity Date, March 1	1
Period of the note in days..	90

2. $30,000 × 10% × 30/365 = $246.58

3. $30,000 × 10% × 60/365 = $493.15

4.
2002

Dec. 1	Cash..	30,000.00	
	Notes Payable		30,000.00
	To record note payable.		

Dec. 31	Interest Expense...	246.58	
	Interest Payable..		246.58
	To record accrued interest at year-end.		

Mar. 1	Notes Payable...	30,000.00	
	Interest Payable..	246.58	
	Interest Expense...	493.15	
	Cash		30,739.73
	To record payment of note plus interest.		

Fundamental Accounting Principles, Tenth Canadian Edition

Exercise 13-11 (15 minutes)

a.

2002			
Dec. 31	Warranty Expense...	4,875	
	Estimated Warranty Liability		4,875
	To record estimated warranty liability;		
	15,000 × ½% = 75 units × $65 = $4,875.		

b.

2002			
Dec. 31	Estimated Warranty Liability	3,380	
	Merchandise Inventory..		3,380
	To record replacement of units under warranty;		
	$65 × 52 = $3,380.		

c. $7,800 + $4,875 − $3,380 = $9,295

d. $4,875

Exercise 13-13 (25 minutes)

1.	Income Taxes Payable (actual)	$31,100
	Total accrued [$2,490 × 12]...	29,880
	Adjustment (additional expense)......................................	$ 1,220

2.

2002			
Jan. 31	Income Tax Expense	2,490	
	Income Taxes Payable..		2,490
	To record accrued income tax and liability.		
Feb. 15	Income Taxes Payable..	2,490	
	Cash		2,490
	Paid instalment		
Dec. 31	Income Tax Expense	1,220	
	Income Taxes Payable..		1,220
	To record adjustment to income taxes owed		

*Exercise 13-15 (20 minutes)

1.
Days in July	31
Minus date of note	15
Days remaining in July	16
Add days in August	31
Add days in September	30
	77
Days to equal 90 days or Maturity Date, October 13	13
Period of the note in days	90

2. $66,442 – $65,000 = $1,442

3.
2002
July 15 Cash.. 65,000
         Discount on Notes Payable...................... 1,442
            Notes Payable.. 66,442
         To record discounted note payable.

Oct. 13 Interest Expense...................................... 1,442
         Notes Payable... 66,442
            Cash... 66,442
            Discount on Notes Payable.............................. 1,442
         To record payment of discounted note.

Fundamental Accounting Principles, Tenth Canadian Edition

PROBLEMS

Problem 13-1B (15 minutes)

	December 31,			
	2002	2003	2004	2005
Current liabilities:				
Current portion of long-term debt..........	$53,868	$59,254	$65,180	$71,698
Interest payable.....................................	25,000	19,613	13,688	7,170
Long-term liabilities:				
Long-term debt......................................	196,132	136,878	71,698	0

Problem 13-3B (40 minutes)

1. Warranty expense for November and December 2002:

	Expense
November (20% × 60 = 12 × $14).........................	$168
December (20% × 140 = 28 × $14)	392
Total	$560

2. Warranty expense for January 2003:

Sales in January	50 units
Warranty percentage (20% × 50 units)	10 units
Warranty expense......................................	× $14
	$ 140

3. Balance of the estimated liability as of December 31, 2002:

Warranty expense for November...	$168	credit
Warranty expense for December	392	credit
Cost of replacing items in December (6 × $14) + (17 × $14)..	(322)	debit
Liability balance...	$238	credit

4. Balance of the estimated liability as of January 31, 2003:

Beginning balance..	$238	credit
Warranty expense for January...	140	credit
Cost of replacing items in January (26 × $14).......................	(364)	debit
Liability balance...	$ 14	credit

5.

2002

Nov. 16	Cash...	2,100.00	
	Sales		2,100.00
	Sold toasters to customers.		
16	Cost of Goods Sold (60 × $14)........................	840.00	
	Merchandise Inventory		840.00
	To record the cost of the November 16 sale.		
30	Warranty Expense...	168.00	
	Estimated Warranty Liability....................		168.00
	To record toaster warranty expense and		
	liability at 10% of the selling price.		
Dec. 10	Estimated Warranty Liability............................	84.00	
	Merchandise Inventory		84.00
	To record the cost of coffee grinder warranty		
	replacements (6 × $14).		
20	Cash (140 × $35)	4,900.00	
	Sales		4,900.00
	Sold toasters to customers.		
20	Cost of Goods Sold (140 × $14).......................	1,960.00	
	Merchandise Inventory		1,960.00
	To record the cost of the December 20 sale.		
Dec. 30	Estimated Warranty Liability............................	238.00	
	Merchandise Inventory		238.00
	To record the cost of toaster warranty		
	replacements (17 × $14).		
31	Warranty Expense...	392.00	
	Estimated Warranty Liability....................		392.00
	To record coffee grinder warranty expense		
	and liability at 10% of the selling price.		

2003

Jan. 6	Cash...	1,750.00	
	Sales		1,750.00
	Sold toasters to customers.		
6	Cost of Goods Sold (50 × $14)........................	700.00	
	Merchandise Inventory		700.00
	To record the cost of the January 6 sale.		

Fundamental Accounting Principles, Tenth Canadian Edition

20	Estimated Warranty Liability	364.00	
	Merchandise Inventory.............................		364.00
	To record the cost of toaster warranty replacements (26 × $14).		
31	Warranty Expense	140.00	
	Estimated Warranty Liability		140.00
	To record toaster warranty expense and liability at 10% of the selling price.		

Chapter 14   Partnerships

EXERCISES

Exercise 14-1 (20 minutes)

1. Keith, Scott, and Brian might first consider organizing their business as a general partnership. However, a problem for the new graduates is that they do not have funds and with no past business experience will probably have trouble getting a business loan. Therefore, instead of a partnership, another option is to incorporate. They can find investors to contribute capital for shares. They can structure the financing so that they remain the major shareholders in the company. Several key advantages to the corporate form is that they will have limited liability and the potential to sell more shares if additional funds are needed. As a corporation any profits will be subject to corporate income tax. Any dividends paid to the shareholders will also be taxed at the individual level. However, any salaries that Keith, Scott, and Brian pay themselves will be tax-deductible expenses. A possible downside however is that a bank is likely to ask for a personal guarantee and then they will actually lose the limited liability feature.

2. The two doctors should form a partnership. A general partnership will have the disadvantage of unlimited liability so they may want to consider a limited liability partnership. The partnership can borrow funds from the bank to obtain the initial needed capital for the business. The advantages of the partnership are ease of formation and owner authority. Also the owners will pay individual taxes on profits from the partnership but the partnership will not be taxed.

3. Matt should consider using a limited partnership. Given his real estate expertise he can manage the day to day activities of the partnership and serve as its general partner. He can raise the necessary capital by admitting limited partners. The advantages to Matt will be the authority over the partnership that he will have as general partner and the ease of raising capital. All partners will pay individual taxes on profits distributed to them but the partnership entity will not pay income tax.

Fundamental Accounting Principles, Tenth Canadian Edition

Exercise 14-3 (30 minutes)

		Share to Newton	Share to Scampi	Total
Plan (a)	$180,000 × 1/2	$90,000	$90,000	$180,000
Plan (b)	($52,000/$130,000) × $180,000	$72,000		$ 72,000
	($78,000/$130,000) × $180,000			
			$108,000	108,000
		$72,000	$108,000	$180,000
Plan (c)	Net income			$180,000
	Salary allowances	$85,000	$65,000	
	Interest allowances:			
	($52,000 × 10%)..................................	5,200		
	($78,000 × 10%)..................................		7,800	
	Total salary and interest......................	$90,200	$72,800	(163,000)
	Balance of income			$ 17,000
	Balance allocated equally:			
	($17,000 × 50%).................................	8,500	8,500	17,000
	Balance of income			$ - 0 -
	Shares of each partner	$98,700	$81,300	$180,000

Exercise 14-5 (25 minutes)

a.

2002

Dec. 31   Income Summary..   30,000
             Bim Curtley, Capital   24,750
               Ray Sauer, Capital...............................   54,750
             To transfer net income of $30,000 from the income
             summary to the partners' capital accounts.

Calculations:

	Sauer	Curtley	Total
Net income.................................			$ 30,000
Salary allowances:			
Sauer...	$65,000		
Interest allowances:			
Sauer (15% on $20,000)	3,000		
Curtley (15% on $100,000)		15,000	
Total salaries and interest allocation	$68,000	$ 15,000	−83,000
Balance of net income over allocated			$(53,000)
Balance allocated on 1:3 ratio:			
Sauer (1/4 × −$53,000)	(13,250)		
Curtley (3/4 × −$53,000)...............		(39,750)	
Total allocated...........................			53,000
Balance of net income...................			$ 0
Allocation to each partner	$54,750	$(24,750)	$ 30,000

b.

Capital account balances:	*Sauer*	*Curtley*
Initial investment.............................	$20,000	$100,000
Withdrawals	(7,000)	(24,000)
Share of income	54,750	(24,750)
Ending balances...............................	$67,750	$ 51,250

Fundamental Accounting Principles, Tenth Canadian Edition

Exercise 14-7 (25 minutes)

July 1	Cash	....	95,000	
	Megan, Capital	....		95,000
	To record admission of Megan			
	[($380,000 + $95,000) × 20%].			

b)

July 1	Cash	....	115,000	
	Megan, Capital	....		99,000
	Hagen, Capital	....		12,000
	Baden, Capital	....		4,000
	To record admission of Megan*.			

> **Supporting computations:*
> *$380,000 + $115,000 = $495,000*
> *$495,000 × 20% = $99,000*
> *$115,000 – $99,000 = $16,000*
> *$ 16,000 × 75% = $12,000*
> *$ 16,000 × 25% = $4,000*

c)

July 1	Cash	....	55,000	
	Hagen, Capital	....	24,000	
	Baden, Capital	....	8,000	
	Megan, Capital	....		87,000
	To record admission of Megan*.			

> **Supporting computations:*
> *$380,000 + $55,000 = $435,000*
> *$435,000 × 20% = $87,000*
> *$ 55,000 – $87,000 = –$32,000*
> *–$ 32,000 × 75% = –$24,000*
> *–$ 32,000 × 25% = –$8,000*

Exercise 14-9 (15 minutes)

a)

Nov.	30	Wood, Capital	50,000	
		Cash...		50,000
		To record retirement of Wood.		

b)

Nov.	30	Wood, Capital	50,000	
		Harris, Capital (3/8 × $10,000)..............................	3,750	
		Evans, Capital (5/8 × $10,000)..............................	6,250	
		Cash...		60,000
		To record retirement of Wood.		

c)

Nov.	30	Wood, Capital	50,000	
		Harris, Capital (3/8 × $5,000)................................		1,875
		Evans, Capital (5/8 × $5,000)................................		3,125
		Cash...		45,000
		To record retirement of Wood.		

Exercise 14-11 (20 minutes)

2004

Jan.	1	Martha Wheaton, Capital...	95,000	
		Sam Dun, Capital..	94,000	
		Cash...		189,000
		To distribute remaining cash to partners.		

	Cash	Building	Accum. Amort., Building	Land	Accounts Payable	Martha Wheaton, Capital	Bess Jones, Capital	Sam Dun, Capital
Account balances								
December 31, 2003............	$ 46,000	$ 206,000	$ 120,000	$ 52,000	$ 32,000	$ 79,000	$(13,000)	$ 86,000
Sale of land and building*............................	+170,000	−206,000	−120,000	− 52,000		+ 16,000	+ 8,000	+ 8,000
Balance	$ 216,000	$ 0	$ 0	$ 0	$ 32,000	$ 95,000	$ (5,000)	$ 94,000
Payment of liabilities	− 32,000				− 32,000			
Balance	$ 184,000	$ 0	$ 0	$ 0	$ 0	$ 95,000	$ (5,000)	$ 94,000
Payment of deficiency	+ 5,000						+$5,000	
Balance	$ 189,000	$ 0	$ 0	$ 0	$ 0	$ 95,000	$ 0	$ 94,000

*$170,000 − ($206,000 − $120,000 + $52,000) = $32,000 gain
  $32,000 × 2/4 or 50% = $16,000 to Wheaton
  $32,000 × ¼ or 25% = $8,000 to each of Jones and Dun

Exercise 14-13 (30 minutes)

1.

	Whiz	Bam	Boom	Total
Initial investments	$115,600	$ 88,600	$95,800	$300,000
Allocation of all losses:				
($300,000 – $30,000)/3	(90,000)	(90,000)	(90,000)	(270,000)
Capital balances	$ 25,600	$ (1,400)	$ 5,800	$ 30,000

2.

Dec. 31	Cash...		1,400	
	Bam, Capital...			1,400
	To record payment of deficiency.			
Dec. 31	Whiz, Capital		25,600	
	Boom, Capital		5,800	
	Cash..			31,400
	To distribute remaining cash.			

3. a)

Dec. 31	Whiz, Capital		700	
	Boom, Capital		700	
	Bam, Capital...			1,400
	To transfer deficiency to other partners.			

b)

Dec. 31	Whiz, Capital		24,900	
	Boom, Capital		5,100	
	Cash..			30,000
	To distribute remaining cash.			

PROBLEMS

Problem 14-1B (50 minutes)

a)

Dec. 31	Income Summary	135,000	
	Paula Jones, Capital...		45,000
	Roy Rogers, Capital...		45,000
	Anne Jackson, Capital		45,000
	To close Income Summary.		

b)

Dec. 31	Income Summary	135,000	
	Paula Jones, Capital...		56,700
	Roy Rogers, Capital...		45,900
	Anne Jackson, Capital		32,400
	To close Income Summary.*		

> *Supporting computations:*
> ($92,400/$220,000) × $135,000 = $56,700
> ($74,800/$220,000) × $135,000 = $45,900
> ($52,800/$220,000) × $135,000 = $32,400

Fundamental Accounting Principles, Tenth Canadian Edition

Problem 14-1B *(continued)*

c)

Dec. 31	Income Summary...		135,000	
	Paula Jones, Capital			68,240
	Roy Rogers, Capital			31,980
	Anne Jackson, Capital....................................			34,780
	To close Income Summary*.			

Supporting calculations:	Jones	Rogers	Jackson	Total
Net income...				$135,000
Salary allowances:				
Paula Jones, Capital...........................	$75,000			
Roy Rogers, Capital...........................		$40,500		
Anne Jackson, Capital			$45,500	
Interest allowances:				
Jones (10% on $92,400)	9,240			
Rogers (10% on $74,800)		7,480		
Jackson (10% on $52,800)			5,280	
Total salaries and interest	$84,240	$47,980	$50,780	183,000
Bal. after interest and salaries				$ (48,000)
Balance allocated equally......................	(16,000)	(16,000)	(16,000)	48,000
Balance of income.................................				$ 0
Shares of the partners	$68,240	$31,980	$34,780	$135,000

Problem 14-3B (40 minutes)

Part 1

	Income (Loss) Sharing Plan	Calculations	Vacon	Masters	Ramos	Total
(a)		$195,000/3...................................	$65,000	$65,000	$65,000	$195,000
(b)		$195,000 × ($116,640/$388,800)	$58,500			
		$195,000 × ($129,600/$388,800)		$65,000		
		$195,000 × ($142,560/$388,800)			$71,500	
		Total allocated	$58,500	$65,000	$71,500	$195,000

Problem 14-3B *(continued)* Part 1

(c)				
Net income..				$195,000
Salary allowances..........................	$35,000	$20,000	$45,000	
Interest allowances:				
10% × $116,640	11,664			
10% × $129,600		12,960		
10% × $142,560			14,256	
Total salary and interest..............				(138,880)
Bal. of income				$ 56,120
Balance allocated equally	18,707	18,707	18,706*	(56,120)
Balance of income........................				$ 0
Shares of partners.......................	$65,371	$51,667	$77,962	$195,000

*Decreased to $18,706 due to rounding.

Part 2

IMR PARTNERSHIP
Statement of Partners' Equity
For Year Ended December 31, 2002

	Vacon	Masters	Ramos	Total
Capital, January 1	$ -0-	$ -0-	$ -0-	$ -0-
Plus:				
Investments by owners	116,640	129,600	142,560	388,800
Net income................................	65,371	51,667	77,962	195,000
Total...	$182,011	$181,267	$220,522	$583,800
Less: Partners' withdrawals	15,000	20,000	23,000	58,000
Capital, December 31.....................	$167,011	$161,267	$197,522	$525,800

Part 3

Dec. 31	Income Summary	195,000	
	Milton Vacon, Capital....................................		65,371
	Milford Masters, Capital		51,667
	Marita Ramos, Capital		77,962
	To close Income Summary.		
Dec. 31	Milton Vacon, Capital..	15,000	
	Milford Masters, Capital	20,000	
	Marita Ramos, Capital	23,000	
	Milton Vacon, Withdrawals		15,000
	Milford Masters, Withdrawals......................		20,000
	Marita Ramos, Withdrawals.........................		23,000
	To close withdrawals accounts.		

Fundamental Accounting Principles, Tenth Canadian Edition

Problem 14-5B (50 minutes)

a)

Nov. 1	Lejeune, Capital..	102,000	
	Devereau, Capital		102,000
	To record admission of Devereau.		

b)

Nov. 1	Lejeune, Capital..	102,000	
	Shulak, Capital...		102,000
	To record admission of Shulak.		

c)

Nov. 1	Lejeune, Capital..	102,000	
	Cash		102,000
	To record withdrawal of Lejeune with no bonus.		

d)

Nov. 1	Lejeune, Capital..	102,000	
	Burke, Capital ($129,000 – $102,000) × 1/3	9,000	
	Comeau, Capital ($129,000 – $102,000) × 2/3	18,000	
	Cash		129,000
	To record withdrawal of Lejeune with bonus.		

e)

Nov. 1	Lejeune, Capital..	102,000	
	Accum. Amortization, Computer Equip........................	45,000	
	Burke, Capital ($33,000* × 1/3).................................		11,000
	Comeau, Capital ($33,000* × 2/3).............................		22,000
	Computer Equipment...		78,000
	Cash		36,000
	To record withdrawal of Lejeune with bonus to old partners.		

*$102,000 – ($78,000 – $45,000 + $36,000) = $33,000

Chapter 15   Corporations

EXERCISES

Exercise 15-1 (15 minutes)

		Corporations	*General Partnerships*
1.	Life	Unlimited	Limited
2.	Owners' liability	Limited	Unlimited
3.	Legal status	Separate legal entity	Not separate from partners
4.	Tax status of income	Can be taxed twice	Taxed only once
5.	Owners' authority	One vote per share	Mutual agency
6.	Ease of formation	Requires government approval	Requires only an agreement
7.	Transferability of ownership	High	Low
8.	Ability to raise large amounts of capital	High	Low

Fundamental Accounting Principles, Tenth Canadian Edition

Exercise 15-3 (25 minutes)

a)

Jan.	1	Organization Costs	8,000.00	
		Common Shares................................		8,000.00
		To record issuance of shares.		
	5	Cash	135,000.00	
		Common Shares................................		135,000.00
		To record issuance of shares, 15,000 × $9		
	10	Cash	31,500.00	
		Common Shares................................		31,500.00
		To record issuance of shares.		
	20	Land	43,000.00	
		Common Shares................................		43,000.00
		To record issuance of shares.		
	31	Income Summary	110,000.00	
		Retained Earnings............................		110,000.00
		To close income summary to retained earnings.		

b)

LINDSAY LTD.
Shareholders' Equity
January 31, 2001

Common shares, unlimited shares authorized, 23,000 shares issued and outstanding..............	$217,500
Retained earnings...	110,000
Total shareholders' equity	$327,500

c) Average Issue Price $217,500 ÷ 23,000 shares = $9.46 per share.

Exercise 15-5 (15 minutes)

a.	Organization Costs..	30,000	
	Common Shares...		30,000
	Issued shares to promoters.		
b.	Cash...	70,000	
	Common Shares...		70,000
	Issued common shares for cash.		
c.	Cash...	120,000	
	Preferred Shares		120,000
	Issued preferred shares for cash.		

Exercise 15-7 (10 minutes)

July 25	Building..	240,000	
	Land...	60,000	
	Common Shares...		300,000
	Issued common shares for building and land.		

Fundamental Accounting Principles, Tenth Canadian Edition

Exercise 15-9

1. $4.5 Cumulative Preferred Shares:
   $4.5/share × 40,000 shares = $180,000 each year × 3 years = $540,000

   $12 Noncumulative Preferred Shares:
   $12/share × 8,000 shares = $96,000

   Common Shares:
   $736,000 – (540,000 + 96,000) = $100,000

2. Dec 31/01 Retained Earnings Balance + 2002 Net Income of $1,500,000 – 2002 Dividends of $736,000 = Dec 31/02 Retained Earnings Balance of $890,000

   Therefore,

   Dec 31/01 Retained Earnings Balance = $126,000

OR

	Retained Earnings		
		X	Bal. Dec. 31/01
2002 dividends	736,000	*1,500,000*	2002 net income
		890,000	Bal. Dec. 31/02

3.

MARITIME INC.
Statement of Retained Earnings
For Year Ended December 31, 2002

Retained earnings, January 1..	$ 126,000
Add: Net income	1,500,000
Total	$1,626,000
Less: Cash dividends..	736,000
Retained earnings, December 31	$ 890,000

Exercise 15-11

1. $5/share × 8,000 shares = $40,000

2. $40,000 × 2 years = $80,000

3. a) ($5 × 8,000 shares) = $40,000 × 3 years = $120,000

   b) $4 × 45,000 = $180,000

4. 105,000 + 340,000 − 120,000 − 180,000 = 145,000

5. 160,000 + 450,000 = 610,000

6. 610,000 + 145,000 = 755,000

7. 10,000 − 8,000 = 2,000

8. $160,000/8,000 shares = $20/share

Exercise 15-13 (20 minutes)

NOTE: The holders of the noncumulative preferred shares are entitled to no more than $188,000 of dividends in any year ($4 × 47,000 shares).

	Preferred	Common
2001 ($0):		
Preferred—current..	$ 0	
Common—remainder...		$ 0
Total for the year...	$ 0	$ 0
2002 ($200,000):		
Preferred—current..	$ 188,000	
Common—remainder (200,000 − 188,000).............		$ 12,000
Total for the year...	$ 188,000	$ 12,000
2003 ($420,000):		
Preferred—current..	188,000	
Common—remainder (420,000 − 188,000).............		$232,000
Total for the year...	$ 188,000	$232,000
2004 ($200,000):		
Preferred—current..	$ 188,000	
Common—remainder (200,000 − 188,000).............		$ 12,000
Total for the year...	$ 188,000	$ 12,000
Total for four years...	$ 564,000	$256,000

Exercise 15-15

a) (15,000 shares × $4.50/share) × 2 years = $135,000

b) $150,000 Total dividends – $135,000 paid to preferred shareholders = $15,000 to common shareholders

Exercise 15-17

a)

			Debit	Credit
Oct. 1	Cash		4,000	
	Preferred Shares			4,000
	(1,000 shares × $4.00/share)			
10	Cash		150,000	
	Common Shares			150,000
	(50,000 shares × $3.00/share)			
12	Organization Costs		11,250	
	Preferred Shares			11,250
	(2,500 shares × $4.50/share)			
15	Land		155,000	
	Cash			55,000
	Notes Payable			100,000
20	Cash		70,500	
	Preferred Shares			70,500
24	Cash Dividends Declared (or Retained Earnings)		31,650	
	Common Dividends Payable			22,400
	Preferred Dividends Payable			9,250
	(18,500 preferred shares × $0.50 = $9,250)			
31	Cash		750,000	
	Revenues			750,000
31	Expenses		250,000	
	Cash			250,000
31	Income Summary		500,000	
	Retained Earnings			500,000
31	Retained Earnings*		31,650	
	Dividends			31,650

(*or no entry if on Oct. 24 it was charged to
Retained Earnings.)

Exercise 15-17 *(continued)*

b)

ABC INC.
Balance Sheet
October 31, 2001

Assets

Current assets:

Cash		$669,500
Capital assets:		
Organization costs	$ 11,250	
Land	155,000	
Total capital assets		166,250
Total assets		$835,750

Liabilities

Current liabilities

Dividends payable	$ 31,650	
Long term note payable..........................	100,000	
Total liabilities...		$131,650

Shareholders' Equity

Contributed Capital:

Preferred shares, $0.50 cumulative, 100,000 shares authorized, 18,500 shares issued and outstanding:	$ 85,750	
Common shares, 500,000 shares authorized, 50,000 shares issued and outstanding:	150,000	
Total contributed capital.............................	$235,750	
Retained earnings	468,350	
Total shareholders' equity...........................		704,100
Total liabilities and shareholders' equity		$835,750

*Exercise 15-19 (20 minutes)

a.

Total shareholders' equity		$ 792,500
Less equity applicable to preferred shares:		
Call price ($30 × 5,000)...	$150,000	
Cumulative dividends in arrears (none)	0	(150,000)
Equity applicable to common shares..................................		$ 642,000
Book value of preferred shares ($150,000/5,000).................	$ 30.00	
Book value of common shares ($642,500/40,000)................		$ 16.06

b.

Total shareholders' equity		$ 792,500
Less equity applicable to preferred shares:		
Call price ($30 × 5,000)...	$150,000	
Cumulative dividends in arrears		
(3 × $1.50 × 5,000)	22,500	(172,500)
Equity applicable to common shares..................................		$ 620,000
Book value of preferred shares ($172,500/5,000).................	$ 34,50	
Book value of common shares ($620,000/40,000)................		$ 15.50

Fundamental Accounting Principles, Tenth Canadian Edition

PROBLEMS

Problem 15-1B (40 minutes)

JENSTAR INC
Balance Sheet
October 31, 2001

Assets

Current assets:

Cash	$ 355,000
Accounts receivable	225,000
Office supplies..	85,000
Prepaid insurance	17,000
Total current assets	$ 682,000

Capital assets:
 Property, plant, and equipment:

Land		$1,000,000
Building...	$2,875,000	
Less: Accumulated amortization..................	833,000	2,042,000
Machinery...	$1,600,000	
Less: Accumulated amortization	763,000	837,000
Total capital assets		3,879,000
Total assets		$4,561,000

Liabilities

Current liabilities:

Accounts payable...	$ 158,000	
Wages payable...	130,000	
Unearned fees..	28,000	
Total current liabilities		$ 316,000
Long term liabilities (due in 2001)		550,000
Total liabilities...		$ 866,000

Shareholders' Equity

Contributed Capital:

Preferred Shares, $1.50 non-cumulative, unlimited shares authorized, 30,000 shares issued and outstanding..........	$1,200,000[1]	
Common Shares, unlimited shares authorized, 50,000 shares issued and outstanding...........	1,600,000[2]	
Total contributed capital...............................		$2,800,000
Retained earnings		895,000
Total shareholders' equity..............................		3,695,000
Total liabilities and shareholders' equity		$4,561,000

1. 30,000 preferred shares × $40/share = $1,200,000
2. 50,000 common shares × $32/share = $1,600,000

Problem 15-2B (20 minutes)

Retained earnings December 31, 2001..		$1,960,720
Reductions in retained earnings due to transactions:		
Cash dividends declared:		
Feb. 11, on 350,000 shares (350,000 × $0.25)..........................	$ 87,500	
May 24, on 350,000 shares...	87,500	
Aug. 13, on 365,000 shares (365,000 × $0.25)	91,250	
Dec. 12, on 385,000 shares (385,000 × $0.25)........................	96,250	362,500
Less: Retained earnings December 31, 2002		2,200,500
Net income		$ 602,280

Problem 15-3B (25 minutes)

Immediately after the conversion of preferred shares, the shareholders' equity section would still show 2,000 shares of preferred shares authorized and issued, but only 1,000 shares outstanding. The amount of preferred shares would change from $200,000 to $100,000. Common shares would show 100,000 shares authorized, and 68,000 shares issued. The amount of common shares would be $700,000 instead of $600,000. Retained earnings would not be affected. Total shareholders' equity also would not be affected because $100,000 has simply shifted from the preferred share section to the common share section.

As a common shareholder, you would not want the conversion of preferred shares to take place. As a result of the conversion, a smaller total dividend would be paid to preferred shares and a larger total dividend would be paid to common shares. However, the dividend per common share is less because there are more common shares dividing the cash. Before the conversion, there are 2,000 shares of $11 preferred. Therefore, $22,000 of the $487,000 paid out in dividends goes to the preferred shareholders. If the remaining $465,000 is divided by 60,000 shares of common shares outstanding, the common dividend per share is $7.75. However, after the conversion, $11,000 of the $487,000 paid out in dividends goes to the 1,000 shares of $11 preferred, and the remaining $476,000 is divided between the 68,000 common shares outstanding. This reduces the dividend per share to $7.00.

Problem 15-4B (25 minutes)

1. A = $20/share × 45,000 shares = $900,000

2. B = $3,800,000/$100 per share = 38,000 shares

3. C = 265,000 shares × $5/share = $1,325,000

4. D = 900,000 + 3,800,000 + 1,325,000 = $6,025,000

5. E = 2,500,000 + 1,750,000 + 1,300,000 − 2,200,000 − 1,200,000 = $2,150,000

6. F = 6,025,000 + 2,150,000 = 8,175,000

7. 3 years (1999, 2000, 2001) × ($8 per share × 45,000 shares) = $1,080,000

Problem 15-5B (20 minutes)

a)

Year	Dividends Declared and Paid	Preferred Dividends	Common Dividends
1999	600,000	480,000	120,000
2000	100,000	100,000	0
2001	250,000	250,000	0
2002	1,500,000	1,090,000	410,000

b)

Year	Dividends Declared and Paid	Preferred Dividends	Common Dividends
1999	600,000	480,000	120,000
2000	100,000	100,000	0
2001	250,000	250,000	0
2002	1,500,000	480,000	1,020,000

Problem 15-6B (60 minutes)

1. Journal entries:

Mar. 2	Cash Dividends Declared or Retained Earnings	150,000.00	
	Common Dividend Payable		150,000.00
	Declared dividend on 100,000 outstanding shares.		
31	Common Dividend Payable	150,000.00	
	Cash		150,000.00
	Paid cash dividend.		
Nov. 11	Cash (12,000 × $13)	156,000.00	
	Common shares, ...		156,000.00
	Issues common shares.		
25	Cash (8,000 × $9.50)	76,000.00	
	Common shares		76,000.00
	Issued common shares.		
Dec. 1	Cash Dividends Declared or Retained Earnings	300,000.00	
	Common Dividend Payable		300,000.00
	Declared dividend on 120,000 outstanding shares.		
Dec. 31	Income Summary	536,000.00	
	Retained Earnings		536,000.00
	Closed the Income Summary account.		
31	Retained Earnings	450,000.00	
	Cash Dividends Declared		450,000.00
	Closed the dividends declared account.		

Part 2

CALDWELL CORP.
Statement of Retained Earnings
For Year Ended December 31, 2002

Retained earnings, January 1	$1,080,000
Add: Net income	536,000
Total	$1,616,000
Less: Cash dividends	450,000
Retained earnings, December 31	$1,166,000

Fundamental Accounting Principles, Tenth Canadian Edition

Problem 15-6B (continued)

Part 3

CALDWELL CORP.
Shareholders' Equity
December 31, 2002

Common shares, unlimited shares authorized, 120,000 shares issued and outstanding	$1,032,000
Retained earnings	1,166,000
Total shareholders' equity	$2,198,000

Problem 15-7B (60 minutes)

Part 1

2000

Feb.	5	Cash (70,000 × $10)...	700,000.00	
		Common Shares...		700,000.00
		Issued common shares.		
	28	Organization Costs	40,000.00	
		Common Shares...		40,000.00
		Issued common shares to corporation's promoters.		
Mar.	3	Land	80,000.00	
		Buildings	210,000.00	
		Machinery...	155,000.00	
		Common shares...		445,000.00
		Issues common shares for land, buildings, machinery.		
Dec.	31	Retained Earnings...	27,000.00	
		Income Summary...		27,000.00
		Closed the Income Summary account.		

2001

Jan.	28	Cash (4,000 × $100)...	400,000.00	
		Preferred Shares...		400,000.00
		Issues preferred shares.		
Dec.	31	Income Summary	98,000.00	
		Retained Earnings		98,000.00
		Closed the Income Summary account.		

Problem 15-7B *(continued)*

Part 1

2002

Jan. 1	Cash Dividends Declared or Retained Earnings .	63,550.00	
	Preferred Dividend Payable...........................		40,000.00
	Common Dividend Payable		23,550.00

Preferred dividend = 4,000 × $10 = 40,000,
No. of common shares = 70,000 + 3,750 +
44,000 = 117,750
Common dividend = $0.20 × 117,750 = $23,550

Feb. 5	Preferred Dividend Payable................................	40,000.00	
	Common Dividend Payable	23,550.00	
	Cash..		63,550.00
	Paid dividends.		

Dec. 31	Retained Earnings	63,550.00	
	Cash Dividends Declared...........................		63,550.00
	Closed dividends.		

31	Income Summary..	159,000.00	
	Retained Earnings...		159,000.00
	Closed the Income Summary account.		

Part 2

SOLAR ENERGY COMPANY INC.
Statement of Retained Earnings
For Year Ended December 31, 2002

Retained earnings, January 1	$ 71,000
Add: Net income	159,000
Total	$230,000
Less: Cash dividends...	63,550
Retained earnings, December 31	$166,450

Fundamental Accounting Principles, Tenth Canadian Edition

Problem 15-7B *(continued)*

Part 3

SOLAR ENERGY COMPANY INC.
Shareholders' Equity
December 31, 2002

Contributed capital:
Preferred, $10, noncumulative, unlimited shares
authorized, 4,000 issued and outstanding........................ $ 400,000
Common shares, unlimited shares authorized,
117,750 shares issued and outstanding 1,185,000
Total contributed capital $1,585,000
Retained earnings 166,450
Total shareholders' equity $1,751,450

Problem 15-8B (60 minutes)

1.

Jan.	1 Cash (130,000 × $4.75)	617,500	
	Common shares		617,500
	Issued common shares.		
	5 Cash Dividends Declared or Retained Earnings	270,000	
	Preferred Dividend Payable (100,000 × $0.75)		75,000
	Common Dividend Payable (270,000 – 75,000)......		195,000
	Declared dividend on preferred and common shares.		
Feb.	28 Preferred Dividend Payable..	75,000	
	Common Dividend Payable	195,000	
	Cash...		270,000
	Paid cash dividends.		
July	1 Cash	675,000	
	Preferred Shares...		675,000
	Issued preferred shares.		
Sept.	5 Cash Dividend Declared or Retained Earnings	307,500	
	Preferred Dividend Payable ($0.75 × 150,000)		112,500
	Common Dividend Payable ($0.25 × 780,000)........		195,000
	Declared dividend on preferred and common shares.		
Oct.	28 Preferred Dividend Payable..	112,500	
	Common Dividend Payable...................................	195,000	
	Cash...		307,500
	Paid cash dividends declared.		

Problem 15-8B *(continued)*

Dec. 31 Retained Earnings...	577,500	
Cash Dividends Declared		577,500
Closed the dividend account.		
Retained Earnings...	480,000	
Income Summary...		480,000
Closed the Income Summary account.		

2.

FRANCOIS CORP.
Statement of Retained Earnings
For Year Ended December 31, 2001

Retained earnings, January 1		$1,135,000
Less: Net loss	480,000	
Cash dividends..	577,500	1,057,500
Retained earnings, December 31		$ 77,500

3.

FRANCOIS CORP.
Shareholders' Equity
December 31, 2001

Contributed Capital:	
Preferred shares, $0.75 noncumulative, unlimited shares authorized	
150,000 shares issued and outstanding...................	$1,975,000
Common shares, unlimited shares authorized,	
780,000 shares issued and outstanding..................	3,542,500
Total contributed capital..	$5,517,500
Retained earnings...	77,500
Total shareholders' equity...	$5,595,000

Fundamental Accounting Principles, Tenth Canadian Edition

*Problem 15-9B (25 minutes)

a.
Book value per share of preferred is call price......................	$ 106.00
Total shareholders' equity..	$920,000
Less total book value of preferred ($106 × 2,000)...................	212,000
Total book value of common...	$708,000
Book value per share of common ($708,000/60,000).............	$ 11.80

b.
Call price	$ 106.00
Dividends in arrears	11.00
Book value per share of preferred	$ 117.00
Total shareholders' equity..	$920,000
Less total book value of preferred ($117 × 2,000)...................	234,000
Total book value of common...	$686,000
Book value per share of common ($686,000/60,000).............	$ 11.43

c.
Call price	$ 106.00
Dividends in arrears ($11 × 3)...	33.00
Book value per share of preferred	$ 139.00
Total shareholders' equity	$920,000
Less total book value of preferred ($139,000 × 2,000)...........	278,000
Total book value of common...	$642,000
Book value per share of common ($642,000/60,000).............	$ 10.70

*Problem 15-10B (25 minutes)

Part 1:

a.

Book value per common share	Book value per preferred share
$\dfrac{1,800,000 - [400,000 + (\$0.75 \times 50,000 \times 2 \text{ years})]}{125,000}$ $= \underline{\$10.60}$	$\dfrac{400,000 \times (\$0.75 \times 50,000 \times 2 \text{ years})}{50,000}$ $= \underline{\$9.50}$

b.

Book value per common share	Book value per preferred share
$\dfrac{1,800,000 - 400,000}{125,000}$ $= \underline{\$11.20}$	$\dfrac{400,000}{50,000}$ $= \underline{\$8.00}$

Part 2:

c.

Book value per common share	Book value per preferred share
$\dfrac{1,800,000 - (400,000 + 25,000^*)}{125,000}$ $= \underline{\$11.00}$ * $\$0.75 \times 50,000 \times 2 \text{ years} = \$74,000;$ $\$75,000 - \$50,000$ dividends paid $= \$25,000$ arrears	$\dfrac{400,000 + 25,000}{50,000}$ $= \underline{\$8.50}$

d.

Book value per common share	Book value per preferred share
$\dfrac{1,800,000 - 400,000}{125,000}$ $= \underline{\$11.20}$	$\dfrac{400,000}{50,000}$ $= \underline{\$8.00}$

Part 3:

e.

Book value per common share	Book value per preferred share
$\dfrac{1,800,000 - (\$12 \times 50,000)}{125,000}$ $= \underline{\$9.60}$	$\dfrac{\$12 \times 50,000}{50,000}$ $= \underline{\$12.00}$

Fundamental Accounting Principles, Tenth Canadian Edition

Chapter 16

Corporate Reporting: Income, Earnings per Share, and Retained Earnings

EXERCISES

Exercise 16-1 (30 minutes)

WESSON COMPANY LTD.
Income Statement
For Year Ended December 31, 2001

Sales		$700,240
Cost and expenses:		
Cost of goods sold	$420,200	
Salaries expense	66,700	
Amortization expense	62,100	
Income from continuing operations before income tax		
Income tax expense	68,380	617,380
Income from continuing operations		$ 82,860
Discontinued operations:		
Loss from operating division (net of $10,200 tax benefit)	$(24,000)	
Gain on sale of division C (net of $19,700 income tax)	66,000	42,000
Income before extraordinary items		$124,860
Extraordinary items:		
Extraordinary gain on provincial condemnation of land		
(net of $24,800 income tax)		68,000
Net income		$192,860

Exercise 16-3 (10 minutes)

1. A. Income from continuing operations
2. C. Gain or loss from disposing of a discontinued operation
3. B. Income from operating a discontinued operation
4. A. Income from continuing operations
5. A. Income from continuing operations
6. D. Extraordinary gain or loss
7. A. Income from continuing operations
8. A. Income from continuing operations

Exercise 16-5 (20 minutes)

2002

Oct. 31
Common Shares..	40,000	
Retained Earnings......................................	4,000	
Cash..		44,000

To record the retirement of 800 shares; $250,000/5,000 shares = $50 average issue price per share × 800 shares = $40,000; 800 × $55 = $44,000.

SANBORN CORPORATION
Shareholders' Equity
October 31, 2002

Common shares, unlimited number of shares authorized, 4,200 shares issued and outstanding	$210,000
Retained earnings	216,000
Total shareholders' equity	$426,100

Exercise 16-7 (40 minutes)

FARGO INC.
Shareholders' Equity
December 31, 2002

Contributed Capital:	
Common shares, 2,000,000 shares authorized, 700,000 shares issued, 400,000 shares outstanding................................	$1,000,000
Retained earnings..	880,000
Total shareholders' equity	$1,880,000

Calculations:

	Number of Common Shares Outstanding	Dollars	Retained Earnings	Total Shareholders' Equity
Balance at December 31, 2001.....	500,000	$1,250,000	$640,000	$1,890,000
Share sales	200,000	500,000	-	500,000
Totals..	700,000	$1,750,000	$640,000	$2,390,000
Share repurchase.........................	(300,000)	(750,000)*	(75,000)	(825,000)
Totals..	400,000	$1,000,000	$565,000	$1,565,000
Cash dividends............................	-	-	(175,000)	(175,000)
Net income.................................	-	-	490,000	490,000
Balance at December 31, 2002.....	400,000	$1,000,000	$880,000	$1,880,000

* $1,750,000/700,000 shares = $2.50 average issue price per share
$2.50 × 300,000 shares = $750,000

Exercise 16-9 (40 minutes)

a.

2002			
Apr. 1	Common Shares (280,000 × $5.00*)	1,400,000	
	Retained Earnings	70,000	
	Cash (280,000 × $5.25).................................		1,470,000
	To record retirement of shares.		
	*$3,400,000/680,000 = $5.00 average issue price.		

Dec. 1	No entry.		
	680,000 – 280,000 = 400,000 × 2 = 800,000 shares.		

31	Income Summary...	810,000	
	Retained Earnings		810,000
	To close income summary to retained earnings.		

Exercise 16-9 (continued)

JETSET INC.
Shareholders' Equity*
December 31, 2002

Common shares, unlimited shares authorized, 800,000 shares issued and outstanding	$2,000,000
Retained earnings	2,540,000
Total shareholders' equity	$4,540,000

Calculations:

	Common Shares — Number of Common Shares Outstanding	Common Shares — Dollars	Retained Earnings	Total Shareholders' Equity
Balance at December 31, 2001	680,000	$3,400,000	$1,800,000	$5,200,000
Share repurchase	(280,000)	(1,400,000)	70,000	(1,470,000)
Totals	400,000	$2,000,000	$1,730,000	$3,730,000
Stock dividend	× 2	0	0	0
Totals	800,000	$2,000,000	$1,730,000	$3,730,000
Net income	-	-	810,000	810,000
Balance at December 31, 2002	800,000	$2,000,000	$2,540,000	$4,540,000

Exercise 16-11 (15 minutes)

Earnings per share:

	Basic
Income before discontinued operations and extraordinary items ($153,000/100,000)	$1.53
Loss from discontinued operations ($78,000/100,000)	(0.78)
Extraordinary gain ($43,200/100,000)	0.43
Net Income ($118,200/100,000)	$1.18

Exercise 16-13 (20 minutes)

Basic earnings per share:

$$\text{Basic EPS} = \frac{\text{Net Income} - \text{Preferred Dividends}}{\text{Weighted-Avg Common Shares Outstanding}}$$

= ($741,500 – $66,500) / 150,001*

= $4.50 per share

*Calculations:

Time Period	Outstanding Shares	Effect of Split	Fraction of Year	Weighted Average*
January – February	60,000	× 2	× 2/12	= 20,000
March – July.................·.............	80,000	× 2	× 5/12	= 66,667
August – November	76,000	× 2	× 4/12	= 50,667
December	152,000		× 1/12	= 12,667
Weighted average outstanding shares....				150,001

*Rounded to nearest whole share.

Exercise 16-15 (30 minutes)

a.

Net income	$480,000
Less: Preferred dividends	65,000
Earnings available to common shareholders......................	$415,000

b.

Time Period	Original Shares	Effect of Split	Post-Split Shares
January – May	50,000	× 3	= 150,000
June – August	80,000	× 3	= 240,000
September – December	67,000	× 3	= 201,000

Time Period	Outstanding Shares	Fraction of Year	Weighted Average
January – May	150,000	× 5/12	= 62,500
June – August	240,000	× 3/12	= 60,000
September – December	201,000	× 4/12	= 67,000
Weighted-average outstanding shares......			189,500

c.

Earnings available to common shareholders......................	$415,000
Divided by weighted-average outstanding shares	189,500
Basic earnings per share..	$2.19

Exercise 16-17 (10 minutes)

The income statement for 2003 and thereafter will report amortization expense of $33,750 (= ($225,000 − $22,500)/6).

The beginning balance of Retained Earnings for 2003 will report an adjustment of the after-tax cumulative effect of the change in amortization.

*Exercise 16-19

AFFILIATED SYSTEMS, INC. Shareholders' Equity October 10, 2002	
Common shares, unlimited shares authorized, 36,000 shares issued, 31,500 outstanding	$468,000
Retained earnings, of which $135,000 is restricted by treasury shares purchased	432,000
Total	$900,000
Less: Treasury shares	135,000
Total shareholders' equity	$765,000

*Exercise 16-21 (15 minutes)

June 30	Treasury Shares	600,000.00	
	Cash		600,000.00
	Purchased treasury shares.		
Aug. 31	Cash	20,000.00	
	Treasury Shares		20,000.00
	Reissued treasury shares at cost.		
25	Cash	330,000.00	
	Treasury Shares		300,000.00
	Contributed Capital, Treasury Shares		30,000.00
	Reissued treasury shares above cost.		

PROBLEMS

Problem 16-1B (60 minutes)

Part 1

Effect of income taxes (losses in parentheses):

	Pre-tax	25%	After-Tax
c. Cumulative effect of change in accounting principle ...	$46,000	$(11,500)	$34,500
f. Loss on condemnation of property	(32,000)	8,000	(24,000)
m. Loss from operating a discontinued operation	(60,000)	15,000	(45,000)
o. Correction of overstatement of prior year's expense	24,000	(6,000)	18,000
q. Loss on sale of discontinued operation's assets	(90,000)	22,500	(67,500)

Part 2   Income from continuing operations:

d. Sales		$1,320,000
b. Interest earned..		10,000
k. Gain from settling a lawsuit		34,000
Total revenues and gains		$1,364,000
p. Cost of goods sold	$520,000	
i. Amortization expense, equipment	50,000	
n. Amortization expense, buildings	78,000	
h. Other operating expenses...	164,000	
l. Loss on sale of office equipment	12,000	
j. Loss from settling a lawsuit	18,000	
Total expenses and losses......................................		842,000
Income before income taxes.....................................		$ 522,000
e. Income taxes expense (25%).....................................		(130,500)
Income from continuing operations............................		$ 391,500

Part 3   Income from discontinued operation:

m. Loss from operating a discontinued operation (after-tax)	$ (45,000)
q. Loss on sale of discontinued operation's assets (after-tax)..................................	(67,500)
Loss from discontinued operation	$ (112,500)

Part 4   Income before extraordinary items:

Income from continuing operations.............................	$ 391,500
Loss from discontinued operation...............................	(112,500)
Income before extraordinary items	$ 279,000

Part 5   Net income:

Income before extraordinary item	$ 279,000

f. **Extraordinary item:**
   Loss on condemnation of property (after-tax)................ (24,000)
   Net income.. $ 255,000

Problem 16-2B (60 minutes)

Part 1

a.   2000 weighted-average shares:

Time Period	Outstanding Shares	Effect of Dividend	Fraction of Year	Weighted Average
January – June	10,000	× 1.2	× 6/12	= 6,000
July – September..........................	9,000	× 1.2	× 3/12	= 2,700
October – November.....................	12,500	× 1.2	× 2/12	= 2,500
December	15,000		× 1/12	= 1,250
Weighted average outstanding shares....				12,450

b.   2001 weighted-average shares:

Time Period	Outstanding Shares	Fraction of Year	Weighted Average
January – March............................	15,000	× 3/12	= 3,750
April – September	19,000	× 6/12	= 9,500
October – December	17,500	× 3/12	= 4,375
Weighted average outstanding shares....			17,625

c.   2002 weighted-average shares:

Time Period	Outstanding Shares	Effect of Split	Fraction of Year	Weighted Average
January – June	17,500	× 2	× 6/12	= 17,500
July – September..........................	20,500	× 2	× 3/12	= 10,250
October..	18,750	× 2	× 1/12	= 3,125
November – December	37,500		× 2/12	= 6,250
Weighted average outstanding shares....				37,125

Problem 16-2B *(continued)*

Part 2

Earnings Per Share	2002	2001	2000
Income from continuing operations...................................	$3.50	$4.82	$7.23
Loss from discontinued operation......................................	-	-	(2.10)
Income before extraordinary item	$3.50	$4.82	$5.13
Extraordinary item...	(1.00)	0.80	-
Net income	$2.50	$5.62	$5.13

Problem 16-3B (35 minutes)

1, Both the numerator and the denominator are incorrect in Computex's calculation of earnings per share for 2001. The numerator is incorrect because the $45,000 (18,000 × $2.50) preferred dividend should have been subtracted from net income. Because the preferred shares are cumulative, it does not matter that the dividend was not actually declared. The denominator is incorrect for two reasons. First, the outstanding preferred shares should not have been included. Second, the denominator includes the common shares outstanding as of balance sheet date instead of the weighted-average number of common shares outstanding for the year. In other words, the March sale of shares was included as if it had been outstanding all year. The denominator should have been calculated as (108,000 × 3/12) + (132,000 × 9/12) = 126,000.

2. If the preferred shares were noncumulative, the numerator should include the entire $600,000 net income since no cash dividends were declared during the year. In the denominator, if the 24,000 shares issued on March 31 had been a stock dividend, the 108,000 shares outstanding during the three months prior to the dividend should be adjusted for the dividend. In other words, the denominator should be [(108,000 + 24,000) × 3/12] + [132,000 × 9/12] = 132,000.

Fundamental Accounting Principles, Tenth Canadian Edition

Problem 16-4B (60 minutes)

BOSWORTH INC.
Statement of Income and Retained Earnings
For Year Ended December 31, 2001

Sales		$1,800,000
Less: Sales returns and allowances		14,000
Net sales		$1,786,000
Cost of goods sold		480,000
Gross profit		$1,306,000
Selling and administrative expenses		180,000
Income from continuing operations before tax		$1,126,000
Income tax expense		450,400
Income before discontinued operation		$ 675,600
Discontinued operation:		
Operating income on discontinued operation (net of $254,400 tax)	$381,600	
Gain on sale of discontinued operation (net of $96,000 tax)	144,000	525,600
Income before extraordinary item		$1,201,200
Extraordinary item:		
Extraordinary loss (net of $32,000 benefit)		48,000
Net income		$1,153,200
Retained earnings, January 1		342,000
Less: Dividends for 2001		95,000
Retained earnings, December 31		$1,400,200
Earnings per share of common (200,000 shares outstanding):		
Income before discontinued operation		$2.68[1]
Income from discontinued operations		2.63[2]
Income before extraordinary item		$5.31
Extraordinary loss		(0.24)[3]
Net income		$5.07

1. $[\$675,600 - (\$2 \times 70,000)] / 200,000 = \underline{\$2.68}$
2. $(\$525,600)/200,000 = \underline{\$2.63}$
3. $\$ 48,000/200,000 = \underline{\$(0.24)}$

Problem 16-5B (60 minutes)

Part 1

Journal entries:

Jan. 10	Common Shares, (20,000 × $8).............................	160,000		
	Retained Earnings	80,000		
	Cash..		240,000	
	Purchased and retired common shares.			
Mar. 2	Cash Dividends Declared or Retained Earnings	120,000		
	Common Dividend Payable		120,000	
	Declared dividend on 80,000 outstanding shares.			
31	Common Dividend Payable...............................	120,000		
	Cash..		120,000	
	Paid cash dividend.			

Apr. 10   No entry. 80,000 common shares × 3:1 split = 240,000 common shares outstanding as a result of the split.

Nov. 11	Cash (12,000 × $25).......................................	300,000		
	Preferred Shares		300,000	
	Issued preferred shares.			
Dec. 31	Retained Earnings..	136,000		
	Income Summary......................................		136,000	
	Closed the Income Summary account.			
31	Retained Earnings..	120,000		
	Cash Dividends Declared		120,000	
	Closed the dividends declared account.			

Part 2

CALDWELL CORP.
Statement of Retained Earnings
For Year Ended December 31, 2002

Retained earnings, January 1	$1,080,000
Less: Net loss...	136,000
Cash dividends declared..	120,000
Retired common shares...	80,000
Retained earnings, December 31	$ 744,000

Problem 16-5B (continued)

Part 3

CALDWELL CORP.
Shareholders' Equity
December 31, 2002

Contributed Capital:		
Preferred shares, $2.50 noncumulative, unlimited shares authorized,		
12,000 issued and outstanding		$300,000
Common shares, unlimited shares authorized,		
240,000 shares issued and outstanding		640,000
Total contributed capital..		$ 940,000
Retained earnings		744,000
Total shareholders' equity		$1,684,000

Problem 16-6B (45 minutes)

Part 1

Outstanding shares:

	Feb. 15	May 15	Aug. 15	Nov. 15
Beginning balance	8,500	8,500	8,500	8,500
Less: Retired shares (Mar. 2)...................		(500)	(500)	(500)
Add: Dividend shares (Oct. 4) (12.5% × 8,000)..				1,000
Outstanding shares	8,500	8,000	8,000	9,000

Part 2

Net income:

Retained earnings, beginning balance	$135,000
Less: Dividends:	
Feb. 15...	(3,400)
May 15	(3,200)
Aug. 15	(3,200)
Oct. 4	(42,000)
Nov. 15...	(3,600)
Total before net income	$ 79,600
Add: Net income..	?
Retained earnings, ending balance..................................	$147,600

Therefore, net income = $68,000

*Problem 16-7B (60 minutes)

Part 1

Journal entries:

Jan. 10	Treasury shares, Common (20,000 × $12)	240,000	
	Cash		240,000
	Purchased treasury shares.		
Mar. 2	Cash Dividends Declared or Retained Earnings	120,000	
	Common Dividend Payable		120,000
	Declared dividend on 80,000 outstanding shares.		
31	Common Dividend Payable	120,000	
	Cash		120,000
	Paid cash dividend.		
Nov. 11	Cash (12,000 × $13)	156,000	
	Treasury shares, Common (12,000 × $12)		144,000
	Contributed Capital, Treasury shares (12,000 × $1)		12,000
	Reissued treasury shares.		
25	Cash (8,000 × $9.50)	76,000	
	Contributed Capital, Treasury shares	12,000	
	Retained Earnings	8,000	
	Treasury shares, Common (8,000 × $12)		96,000
	Reissued treasury shares.		
Dec. 1	Cash Dividends Declared or Retained Earnings	250,000	
	Common Dividend Payable		250,000
	Declared dividend on 100,000 outstanding shares.		
31	Income Summary	536,000	
	Retained Earnings		536,000
	Closed the Income Summary account.		
Dec. 31	Retained Earnings	370,000	
	Cash Dividends Declared		370,000
	Closed the dividends declared account.		

Problem 16-7B *(continued)*

Part 2

FRANCOIS CORP.
Statement of Retained Earnings
For Year Ended December 31, 2002

Retained earnings, January 1	$1,080,000
Plus net income for year	536,000
Total	$1,616,000
Less: Cash dividends declared...	370,000
Treasury shares reissuances	8,000
Retained earnings, December 31	$1,238,000

Part 3

FRANCOIS CORP.
Shareholders' Equity
December 31, 2002

Common shares, unlimited shares authorized, 100,000 shares issued	$ 800,000
Retained earnings	1,238,000
Total shareholders' equity	$2,038,000

Chapter 17   Bonds and Long-Term Notes Payable

EXERCISES

When solving the following exercises,

1.   *round all dollar amounts to the nearest whole dollar, and*

2.   *assume that none of the companies uses reversing entries.*

Exercise 17-1 (15 minutes)

a.   Size of interest payment = $300,000 × 8% × 1/2 = $12,000
b.   Journal entries:

Jan. 1	Cash	300,000	
	Bonds Payable		300,000
	Sold bonds at par.		
June 30	Interest Expense	12,000	
	Cash		12,000
	Paid semiannual interest on bonds.		
Dec. 31	Interest Expense..	12,000	
	Cash		12,000
	Paid semiannual interest on bonds.		

Exercise 17-3 (20 minutes)

a.

2002

Oct.	1	Cash..	1,355,625	
		Interest Payable...................................		5,625
		Bonds Payable.....................................		1,350,000
		$1,350,000 x 5% x 1/12 = $5,625		

b.

Nov.	30	Interest Payable..	5,625	
		Bond Interest Expense	11,250	
		Cash..		16,875
		$1,350,000 x 5% x 2/12 = $11,250		

c.

Dec.	31	Bond Interest Expense	5,625	
		Interest Payable...................................		5,625

d.

2003

Feb.	28	Interest Payable..	5,625	
		Bond Interest Expense	11,250	
		Cash..		16,875

Exercise 17-5 (20 minutes)

	a.	b.	c.
PV of face amount of $618,000	$506,603	$527,044	$548,362
PV of interest annuity of $6,180 (= $618,000 x 4% x 3/12)	89,117	90,956	92,850
Total issue price	$595,720	$618,000	$641,213

Calculator keystrokes:
n = 4 years x 4 periods per year = 16
FV = –618,000
PMT = –6,180
(a) i = 5% ÷ 4 periods/year = 1.25
(b) i = 4% ÷ 4 periods/year = 1
(c) i = 3% ÷ 4 periods/year = .75
Compute PV

Exercise 17-7 (25 minutes)

a.   Size of semiannual payment = $150,000 × 8% × 1/2 = $6,000

b.   Number of payments = 15 years × 2 = 30

c.   The 8% contract rate is less than the 10% market rate; therefore, the bonds were issued at a discount.

d.   Estimation of the market price at the issue date:

Cash Flow	Table	Table Value	Amount	Present Value
Par value	IV-1	0.2314	$150,000	$ 34,710
Interest (annuity)	IV-3	15.3725	6,000	92,235
Total				$126,945

The table values are based on a discount rate of 5% (half the annual market rate) and 30 periods/payments.

e.   Cash   126,945
     Discount on Bonds Payable   23,055
        Bonds Payable   150,000
        Sold bonds at a discount on the original issue date.

Exercise 17-9 (30 minutes)

a.   Discount = Par value – Issue price = $30,000 – $28,477 = $1,523

b.   Total interest expense over the life of the bonds:

Amount repaid:
   Six payments of $1,200 .... $ 7,200
   Maturity amount   30,000
   Total repaid $37,200
Less: Amount borrowed   28,477
Total interest expense.................................. $ 8,723

or:

Six payments of $1,200 .... $ 7,200
Add: Discount   1,523
Total interest expense .... $ 8,723

Exercise 17-9 *(continued)*

c.   Amortization table:

Period Ending	(a) Beginning Balance Prior (e)	(b) Debit Interest Expense 5% × (a)	(c) Credit Discount on Bonds (b) – (d)	(d) Credit Cash 4% × $ 30,000	(e) Ending Balance (a) + (c)
		Payments			
Jun. 30/02............	$28,477	$ 1,424	$ 224	$ 1,200	$28,701
Dec. 31/02............	28,701	1,435	235	1,200	28,936
Jun. 30/03............	28,936	1,447	247	1,200	29,183
Dec. 31/03............	29,183	1,459	259	1,200	29,442
Jun. 30/04............	29,442	1,472	272	1,200	29,714
Dec. 31/04............	29,714	1,486	286	1,200	30,000
Total		$8,723	$1,523	$7,200	

Exercise 17-11 (30 minutes)

a.

PV of face amount (Table IV.1):	$735,000 × .5470 = $402,045
PV of interest annuity (Table IV.3):...........................	$51,450* × 5.0330 = $258,948
	$660,993

*$735,000 × 7% = $51,450

b.

Period Ending	(a) Cash Interest Paid $735,000 × 7%	(b) Period Interest Expense 434,157/7	(c) Discount Amort. 74,007/7	(d) Unamortized Discount	(e) Carrying Value $735,000 – (d)
Oct. 1/02				74,007	660,993
Oct. 1/03	51,450	62,022	10,572	63,435[1]	671,565
Oct. 1/04	51,450	62,022	10,572	52,863[2]	682,137
Oct. 1/05	51,450	62,022	10,572	42,291[3]	692,709
Oct. 1/06	51,450	62,022	10,572	31,719[4]	703,281
Oct. 1/07	51,450	62,022	10,572	21,147[5]	713,853
Oct. 1/08	51,450	62,022	10,572	10,575[6]	724,425
Oct. 1/09	51,450	62,025*	10,575*	0[7]	735,000
Totals	360,150	434,157	74,007		

*adjusted for rounding

1. 74,007 – 10,572 = 63,435
2. 63,435 – 10,572 = 52,863
3. 52,863 – 10,572 = 42,291
4. 42,291 – 10,572 = 31,719
5. 31,719 – 10,572 = 21,147
6. 21,147 – 10,572 = 10,575
7. 10,575 – 10,575 = 0

Exercise 17-13 (30 minutes)

a.

PV of face amount (Using Table IV.1):	$735,000 × .5835 = $428,873
PV of interest annuity (Using Table IV.3):..................	$51,450* × 5.2064 = $267,869
	$696,742

*$735,000 × 7% = $51,450

Exercise 17-13 (continued)

b.

Period Ending	(a) Cash Interest Paid $735,000 × 7%	(b) Period Interest Expense (e) × 8%	(c) Discount Amort. (b) – (a)	(d) Unamortized Discount 38,258	(e) Carrying Value $735,000 – (d)
Oct. 1/02				38,258	696,742
Oct. 1/03	51,450	55,739[1]	4,289	33,969	701,031
Oct. 1/04	51,450	56,082[2]	4,632	29,337	705,663
Oct. 1/05	51,450	56,453[3]	5,003	24,334	710,666
Oct. 1/06	51,450	56,853[4]	5,403	18,931	716,069
Oct. 1/07	51,450	57,286[5]	5,836	13,095	721,905
Oct. 1/08	51,450	57,752[6]	6,302	6,793	728,207
Oct. 1/09	51,450	58,257[7]	6,793*	0	735,000
Totals	360,150	398,422	38,258		

*adjusted for rounding.

1. 696,742 × 8% = 55,739
2. 701,031 × 8% = 56,082
3. 705,663 × 8% = 56,453
4. 710,666 × 8% = 56,853
5. 716,069 × 8% = 57,286
6. 721,905 × 8% = 57,752
7. 728,207 × 8% = 58,257

Exercise 17-15 (20 minutes)

a. Journal entry

2002

Jan. 1	Cash	294,000	
	Discount on Bonds Payable	6,000	
	Bonds Payable		300,000
	Sold bonds at a discount.		

b. Journal entry

2002

Jan. 1	Cash	306,000	
	Premium on Bonds Payable		6,000
	Bonds Payable		300,000
	Sold bonds at a premium.		

Exercise 17-17 (30 minutes)

a.   Premium = Issue price – Par value = $42,030 – $40,000 = $2,030

b.   Total interest expense over the life of the bonds:

Amount repaid:
Six payments of $2,400	$14,400
Maturity amount	40,000
Total	$54,400
Less: Amount borrowed	42,030
Total interest expense	$12,370

or:

Six payments of $2,400	$14,400
Less	2,030
Total interest expense	$12,370

c.   Amortization table:

Payments

	(a)	(b)	(c)	(d)	(e)
		Debit	Debit		
	Beginning	Interest	Premium	Credit	Ending
	Balance	Expense	+ on Bonds	= Cash	Balance
Period Ending	Prior (e)	5% × (a)	(d) – (b)	6% × $40,000	(a) – (c)
Jun. 30/02	$42,030	$ 2,102	$ 298	$ 2,400	$41,732
Dec. 31/02	41,732	2,087	313	2,400	41,419
Jun. 30/03	41,419	2,071	329	2,400	41,090
Dec. 31/03	41,090	2,055	345	2,400	40,745
Jun. 30/04	40,745	2,037	363	2,400	40,382
Dec. 31/04	40,382	2,018*	382	2,400	40,000
Total		$12,370	$2,030	$14,400	

Adjusted for rounding.

Exercise 17-19 (25 minutes)

Part 1a.

2002

Oct. 1 Cash.. 776,063
            Premium on Bonds Payable 41,063
            Bonds Payable 735,000

b.

Nov. 30 Bond Interest Expense (45,584 × 2/12) 7,597
            Premium on Bonds Payable (5,866 × 2/12).................... 978
               Interest Payable (51,450 × 2/12) 8,575

c.

2003

Oct. 1 Interest Payable... 8,575
            Bond Interest Expense (45,584 × 10/12) 37,987
            Premium on Bonds Payable (5,866 × 10/12).................... 4,888
                Cash... 51,450

Part 2

Long-term liabilities:
    Bonds payable, 7%, due October 1, 2009....................................... $735,000
    Add: Premium on bonds payable.. 16,621*
                                                               $751,621

*$17,599 − ($5,866 × 2/12 = $978) = $16,621

Exercise 17-21 (25 minutes)

Part 1a.
2002

Oct. 1	Cash	820,075	
	Premium on Bonds Payable		85,075
	Bonds Payable		735,000

b.

Nov. 30	Bond Interest Expense (41,004 × 2/12)	6,834	
	Premium on Bonds Payable (10,446 × 2/12)...................	1,741	
	Interest Payable (51,450 × 2/12)............................		8,575

c.
2003

Oct. 1	Interest Payable	8,575	
	Bond Interest Expense (41,004 × 10/12)	34,170	
	Premium on Bonds Payable (10,446 × 10/12).................	8,705	
	Cash		51,450

Part 2
Long-term liabilities:

Bonds payable, 7%, due October 1, 2009	$735,000
Add: Premium on bonds payable...	25,131*
	$760,131

*$27,353 – ($13,332 × 2/12 = $2,222) = $25,131

Exercise 17-23 (20 minutes)

a. The amount of principal in each payment = $16,000/4 pmts. = $4,000

b. Amortization table for the loan:

		Payments			
Period Ending	(a) Beginning Balance Prior (e)	(b) Debit Interest Expense 5% × (a)	(c) Debit Notes + Payable $16,000/4	(d) Credit = Cash (b) + (c)	(e) Ending Balance (a) − (c)
2003	$16,000	$ 800	$ 4,000	$ 4,800	$12,000
2004	12,000	600	4,000	4,600	8,000
2005	8,000	400	4,000	4,400	4,000
2006	4,000	200	4,000	4,200	0
Total		$2,000	$ 16,000	$18,000	

Exercise 17-25 (20 minutes)

a. The size of each payment = Initial note balance/Table IV-2 value
   = $10,000/3.5460 = $2,820

b. Amortization table for the loan:

		Payments			
Period Ending	(a) Beginning Balance Prior (e)	(b) Debit Interest Expense 5% × (a)	(c) Debit Notes + Payable (d) − (b)	(d) Credit = Cash (b) + (c)	(e) Ending Balance (a) − (c)
2003	$10,000	$ 500	$ 2,320	$ 2,820	$7,680
2004	7,680	384	2,436	2,820	5,244
2005	5,244	262	2,558	2,820	2,686
2006	2,686	134	2,686	2,820	0
Total		$1,280	$10,000	$11,280	

*Exercise 17-27 (30 minutes)

a)

Dec. 31	Leased Equipment	22,745	
	Lease liability		22,745

$6,000 × 3.7908

b)

Dec. 31	Interest Expense	2,275	
	Lease liability		2,275

($22,745 × 10%)

c)

Dec. 31	Amortization expense, Equipment................	2,843	
	Accumulated amortization, Equip.		2,843

($22,745/8 years) It is also common to credit
the leased asset account rather than
accumulated amortization.

d)

Dec. 31	Lease liability......................................	6,000	
	Cash.		6,000

e.

(a)	(b)	(c)	(d)	(e)	(f)
Year	Beginning Net liability	Payment	Interest Expense (b) × 10%	Reduction in lease liability (c) – (d)	Lease Liability at End of Year (b) – (e)
2003	$22,745	$6,000	$2,275	$3,725	$19,020
2004	19,020	6,000	1,902	4,098	14,922
2005	14,922	6,000	1,492	4,508	10,414
2006	10,414	6,000	1,041	4,959	5,455
2007	5,455	6,000	545*	5,455	0
Total expense			$7,255		

*Rounding adjustment.

Fundamental Accounting Principles, Tenth Canadian Edition

PROBLEMS

Problem 17-1B (50 minutes)

Part 1

a.

Cash Flow	Table	Table Value	Amount	Present Value
Par value	IV-1	0.4564	$50,000	$ 22,820
Interest (annuity)..........	IV-3	13.5903	2,500	33,976
Total.............................				$56,796
Premium (rounded)......				$ 6,796

The table values are based on a discount rate of 4% (half the annual market rate) and 20 periods/payments.

b.

2002			
Jan. 1	Cash	56,796	
	Premium on Bonds Payable		6,796
	Bonds Payable		50,000
	Sold bonds on the original issue date.		

Part 2

a.

Cash Flow	Table	Table Value	Amount	Present Value
Par value	IV-1	0.3769	$50,000	$ 18,845
Interest (annuity)..........	IV-3	12.4622	2,500	31,155*
Total.............................				$ 50,000

* rounding

The table values are based on a discount rate of 5% (half the annual market rate) and 20 periods/payments. (Note: When the contract rate and market rate are the same, the bonds sell at par and there is no discount or premium.)

b.

2002			
Jan. 1	Cash	50,000	
	Bonds Payable		50,000
	Sold bonds on the original issue date.		

Problem 17-1B *(continued)*

Part 3

a.

Cash Flow	Table	Table Value	Amount	Present Value
Par value........................	IV-1	0.3118	$50,000	$15,590
Interest (annuity)	IV-3	11.4699	2,500	28,675
Total				$44,265
Discount				$ 5,735

The table values are based on a discount rate of 6% (half the annual market rate) and 20 periods/payments.

b.

2002
Jan. 1   Cash... 44,265
     Discount on Bonds Payable........................... 5,735
        Bonds Payable.. 50,000
      Sold bonds on the original issue date.

Problem 17-2B (40 minutes) *Part 1*

a.

Cash Flow	Table	Table Value	Amount	Present Value
Par value........................	IV-1	0.3118	$3,700,000	$1,153,660
Interest (annuity)	IV-3	11.4699	238,650	2,737,292
Total				$3,890,952
Premium				$ 190,952

The table values are based on a discount rate of 6% (half the annual market rate) and 20 periods/payments.

2002
Jan. 1   Cash... 3,890,952
     Premium on Bonds Payable.................... 190,952
     Bonds Payable.. 3,700,000
     Sold bonds on the original issue date at a premium.

Fundamental Accounting Principles, Tenth Canadian Edition

Problem 17-2B *(continued)*

Part 2

Cash Payment = $3,700,000 \times 12.9\% \times 6/12 = \$238,650$

Straight-line premium amortization =

$3,890,952 - 3,700,000 = \$190,952$

$190,952 / 20$ interest payment periods = $\$9,548^*$

*rounded

Bond interest expense = $238,650 - 9,548 = \$229,102$

Part 3

Twenty payments of $238,650	$4,773,000
Maturity amount...	3,700,000
Total repaid	$8,473,000
Less: Amount borrowed	3,890,952
Total bond interest expense	$4,582,048

or:

Thirty payments of $238,650	$4,773,000
Less: Premium	190,952
Total bond interest expense	$4,582,048

Part 4

	(a)	(b)		(c)		(d)	(e)
				Payments			
Period Ending	Beginning Balance Prior (e)	Debit Interest Expense	–	Debit Premium on Bonds $190,952/20	=	Credit Cash 12.9%/2 × $3,700,000	Ending Balance (a) – (c)
Jun.30/02	$3,890,952	$229,102		$9,548		$238,650	$3,881,404
Dec.31/02	3,881,404	229,102		9,548		238,650	3,871,856

Problem 17-2B *(continued)*

Part 5

2002

June 30   Bond Interest Expense   229,102
                 Premium on Bonds Payable   9,548
                      Cash   238,650
                      To record six months' interest and premium
                      amortization.

Dec. 31   Bond Interest Expense   229,102
                 Premium on Bonds Payable   9,548
                      Cash   238,650
                      To record six months' interest and premium
                      amortization.

Part 6

Period Ending	A Beginning Premium Balance	B Amount Amortized*	A – B Ending Premium Balance
June 30/02	190,952	$9,548	.$181,404
Dec. 31/02	181,404	9,548	171,856
June 30/03	171,856	9,548	162,308
Dec. 31/03	162,308	9,548	152,760

*Semiannual amortization: $190,952/20 = $9,548$

Problem 17-3B (50 minutes)

Semiannual interest payment = ($800,000 × 0.097)/2 = $38,800

Present value of $800,000 to be received after 20 periods,
   discounted at 5% per period ($800,000 × 0.3769) $301,520
Present value of $38,800 to be received periodically for 20
   periods discounted at 5% ($38,800 × 12.4622) ....   <u>483,533</u>
Price of the bonds ....   <u>$785,053</u>

2002

Dec. 31   Cash   785,053
                 Discount on Bonds Payable   14,947
                      Bonds Payable   800,000

               Fundamental Accounting Principles, Tenth Canadian Edition

Problem 17-3B *(continued)*

Part 2

20 payments of $38,800	$ 776,000
Maturity amount...	800,000
Total repaid	$1,576,000
Less: Amount borrowed	785,053
Total interest expense...............................	$ 790,947

or:

20 payments of $38,800.............................	$ 776,000
Add: Discount	14,947
Total interest expense...............................	$ 790,947

Part 3

Period Ending	*(a)* Beginning Carrying Amount	*(b)* Interest Expense for the Period (a) × 5%	*(c)* Interest to be Paid the Bondholders	*(d)* Discount to be Amortized (b) – (c)	*(e)* Unamortized Discount at End of Period	*(f)* Ending Carrying Amount $800,000 – (e)
Jun. 30/02	$785,053	$39,253	$38,800	$453	$14,494	$785,506
Dec. 31/02	785,506	39,275	38,800	475	14,019	785,981

Part 4

2003

June 30	Bond Interest Expense...	39,253	
	Discount on Bonds Payable		453
	Cash		38,800
Dec. 31	Bond Interest Expense...	39,275	
	Discount on Bonds Payable		475
	Cash		38,800

Problem 17-4B (30 minutes)

Part 1

a.

PV of face amount (FV = –$625,000; n = 12; I = 11 ÷ 4).............................. $451,334
PV of interest annuity (PMT = –$18,750*; n = 12; I = 11 ÷ 4) 189,454
$640,788

*$625,000 × 12% × 3/12 = $18,750

b.

Period Ending	(a) Cash Interest Paid $625,000 × 12% × 3/12	(b) Period Interest Expense 209,212/12	(c) Premium Amort. 15,788/12	(d) Unamortized Premium 15,788	(e) Carrying Value $625,000 + (d)
May 1/02				15,788	640,788
Aug. 1/02	18,750	17,434	1,316	14,472 [1]	639,472
Nov. 1/02	18,750	17,434	1,316	13,156 [2]	638,156
Feb. 1/03	18,750	17,434	1,316	11,840 [3]	636,840
May 1/03	18,750	17,434	1,316	10,524 [4]	635,524
Aug. 1/03	18,750	17,434	1,316	9,208 [5]	634,208
Nov. 1/03	18,750	17,434	1,316	7,892 [6]	632,892
Feb. 1/04	18,750	17,434	1,316	6,576 [7]	631,576
May 1/04	18,750	17,434	1,316	5,260 [8]	630,260
Aug. 1/04	18,750	17,434	1,316	3,944 [9]	628,944
Nov. 1/04	18,750	17,434	1,316	2,628 [10]	627,628
Feb. 1/05	18,750	17,434	1,316	1,312 [11]	626,312
May 1/05	18,750	17,438*	1,312*	0 [12]	625,000
Totals	225,000	209,212	15,788		

adjusted due to rounding.

1. 15,788 – 1,316 = 14,472
2. 14,472 – 1,316 = 13,156
3. 13,156 – 1,316 = 11,840
4. 11,840 – 1,316 = 10,524
5. 10,524 – 1,316 = 9,208
6. 9,208 – 1,316 = 7,892
7. 7,892 – 1,316 = 6,576
8. 6,576 – 1,316 = 5,260
9. 5,260 – 1,316 = 3,944
10. 3,944 – 1,316 = 2,628
11. 2,628 – 1,316 = 1,312
12. 1,312 – 1,312 = 0

Problem 17-5B (25 minutes)

Part 1
a.

2002				
May 1	Cash..	640,788		
	Premium on Bonds Payable...........................		15,788	
	Bonds Payable...		625,000	

b.

Aug. 1	Bond Interest Expense	17,434	
	Premium on Bonds Payable..............................	1,316	
	Cash		18,750

c.

Aug. 31	Bond Interest Expense (17,434 × 1/3)	5,811	
	Premium on Bonds Payable (1,316 × 1/3)...........	439	
	Interest Payable (18,750 × 1/3)		6,250

d.

Nov. 1	Interest Payable	6,250	
	Bond Interest Expense (17,434 × 2/3)	11,623	
	Premium on Bonds Payable (1,316 × 2/3)	877	
	Cash		18,750

Part 2
Long-term liabilities:

Bonds payable, 12%, due May 1, 2005...	$625,000
Add: Premium on bonds payable...	3,505*
	$628,505

*$3,944 – ($1,316 × 1/3 = $439) = $3,505

Problem 17-6B (30 minutes)

a.

PV of face amount (FV = –$350,000; n = 8; I = 13.5 ÷ 2)............................	$207,551
PV of interest annuity (PMT = –$26,250*; n = 8; I = 13.5 ÷ 2)	158,277
	$365,828

*$350,000 × 15% × 6/12 = $26,250

b.

Period Ending	(a) Cash Interest Paid $350,000 × 15% × 6/12	(b) Period Interest Expense (e) × 13.5% × 6/12	(c) Premium Amort. (b) – (c)	(d) Unamortized Premium	(e) Carrying Value $350,000 + (d)
Sept 1/02				15,828	365,828
Mar. 1/03	26,250	24,693 [1]	1,557	14,271	364,271
Sept. 1/03	26,250	24,588 [2]	1,662	12,609	362,609
Mar. 1/04	26,250	24,476 [3]	1,774	10,835	360,835
Sept. 1/04	26,250	24,356 [4]	1,894	8,941	358,941
Mar. 1/05	26,250	24,229 [5]	2,021	6,920	356,920
Sept. 1/05	26,250	24,092 [6]	2,158	4,762	354,762
Mar. 1/06	26,250	23,946 [7]	2,304	2,458	352,458
Sept. 1/06	26,250	23,792 *[8]	2,458	0	350,000
Totals	210,000	194,172	15,828		

*adjusted for rounding.

1. 365,828 × (13.5% × 6/12) = 24,693
2. 364,271 × (13.5% × 6/12) = 24,588
3. 362,609 × (13.5% × 6/12) = 24,476
4. 360,835 × (13.5% × 6/12) = 24,356
5. 358,941 × (13.5% × 6/12) = 24,229
6. 356,920 × (13.5% × 6/12) = 24,092
7. 354,762 × (13.5% × 6/12) = 23,946
8. 352,458 × (13.5% × 6/12) = 23,792

Fundamental Accounting Principles, Tenth Canadian Edition

Problem 17-7B (25 minutes)

Part 1

a.

2002

Sept . 1 Cash.. 365,828
    Premium on Bonds Payable............................   15,828
    Bonds Payable...   350,000

b.

2003

Jan. 31 Bond Interest Expense (24,693 × 5/6)........................... 20,578
   Premium on Bonds Payable (1,557 × 5/6)..................... 1,297**
    Interest Payable (26,250 × 5/6)   21,875

c.

Mar. 1 Interest Payable.. 21,875
   Bond Interest Expense (24,693 × 1/6)........................... 4,115
   Premium on Bonds Payable (1,557 × 1/6) 260
    Cash...   26,250

Part 2

Long-term liabilities:
 Bonds Payable, 15%, due September 1, 2006.......................... $350,000
 Add: Premium on bonds payable......................................   7,257*
                                 $357,257

* $8,941 – ($2,021 × 5/6 = $1,684) = $7,257
** adjusted for rounding.

Problem 17-8B (45 minutes)

Part 1

Ten payments of $12,800	$128,000
Maturity amount.......................................	320,000
Total repaid..	$448,000
Less: Amount borrowed	347,299
Total bond interest expense....................	$100,701

or:

Ten payments of $12,800	$128,000
Less: Premium	27,299
Total bond interest expense....................	$100,701

Part 2

Period Ending	(a) Cash Interest Paid $320,000 × 8% × 6/12	(b) Period Interest Expense (e) × 6% × 6/12	(c) Premium Amort. (a) – (b)	(d) Unamortized Premium	(e) Carrying Value $320,000 + (d)
Jan. 1/02				27,299	347,299
June 30/02	12,800	10,419	2,381	24,918	344,918
Dec. 31/02	12,800	10,348	2,452	22,466	342,466
June 30/03	12,800	10,274	2,526	19,940	339,940
Dec. 31/03	12,800	10,198	2,602	17,338	337,338
June 30/04	12,800	10,120	2,680	14,658	334,658
Dec. 31/04	12,800	10,040	2,760	11,898	331,898
June 30/05	12,800	9,957	2,843	9,055	329,055
Dec. 31/05	12,800	9,872	2,928	6,127	326,127
June 30/06	12,800	9,784	3,016	3,111	323,111
Dec. 31/06	12,800	9,689*	3,111*	0	320,000
Totals	128,000	100,701	27,299		

*adjusted for rounding

Fundamental Accounting Principles, Tenth Canadian Edition

Problem 17-8B *(continued)*

Part 3

2002

June 30   Bond Interest Expense..   10,419

Premium on Bonds Payable...............................   2,381

Cash..   12,800

To record six months' interest and premium amortization.

2002

Dec. 31   Bond Interest Expense..   10,348

Premium on Bonds Payable...............................   2,452

Interest Payable...   12,800

To record six months' interest and premium amortization.

Part 4

As of December 31, 2004:

Cash Flow	Table	Table Value*	Amount	Present Value
Par value.....................	IV.1	.8885	$320,000	$284,320
Interest (annuity).........	IV.3	3.7171	12,800	47,579
Total.............................				$331,899

The table values are based on a discount rate of 3% (half the annual original market rate) and 4 periods/payments remaining in the life of the bonds.

Comparison to Part 2:

Except for a small rounding difference, this present value ($331,899) equals the carrying value of the bonds in column (e) of the amortization table ($331,898). The balance at any point in time equals the present value of the remaining cash flows using the market rate at the time of issuance.

Problem 17-9B (40 minutes)

Bond Issue 1:
a. Discount

b.
2003
Sept. 1 Cash 623,429
         Discount on Bonds Payable 26,571
             Bonds Payable 650,000

c. 7%

d. Effective interest method

e. $11,375 quarterly

f. 20 interest periods or a 5-year term

g.
Long-term liabilities;
    Bonds payable, 7%, due September 1, 2008 .... $650,000
    Less: Discount on bonds payable* 4,175 $645,825

*4,685 – (1,531 × 1/3) = 4,175

h.
Jan. 1/08 to Feb. 28/08: 12,906 × 2/3 = ... $ 8,604
Mar. 1/08 to May 31/08: 12,937
June 1/08 to Sept. 1/08: 12,967
Total interest expense for year ended December 31, 2008 .... $34,508

i.
2007
Dec. 1 Bond Interest Expense 12,876
         Discount on Bonds Payable 1,501
         Cash 11,375

     1 Bonds Payable 650,000
        Loss on Retirement of Bonds 11,185
            Cash (650,000 × 1.01) 656,500
            Discount on Bonds Payable 4,685

Fundamental Accounting Principles, Tenth Canadian Edition

Problem 17-9B *(continued)*

Bond Issue 2:
a. Premium

b.

2001				
May 1	Cash...	822,267		
	Premium on Bonds Payable...........................		42,267	
	Bonds Payable...		780,000	

c. 11%

d. Straight-line method

e. $42,900 semiannually

f. 16 interest periods or an 8-year term

g.

Long-term liabilities;			
Bonds payable, 11%, due May 1, 2009......................		$780,000	
Add: Premium on bonds payable*		7,040	$787,040

7,921 – (2,642 × 2/6) = 7,040

h.

Jan. 1/08 to Apr. 30/08: 40,258 x 4/6 = ...	$26,839
May 1/08 to Oct. 31/08:	40,258
Nov. 1/08 to Dec. 31/08: 40,263 x 2/6 = ...	13,421
Total interest expense for year ended December 31, 2008......................	$80,518

i.

2007			
Dec. 1	Bond Interest Expense (40,258 x 1/6)............................	6,710	
	Premium on Bonds Payable (2,642 x 1/6)	440	
	Cash (42,900 × 1/6)		7,150
1	Bonds Payable...	780,000	
	Premium on Bonds Payable (7,921 – 440)	7,481	
	Loss on Retirement of Bonds	319	
	Cash (780,000 ×1.01)		787,800

Problem 17-10B (60 minutes) *Part 1*

In appendix Table IV-3, the present value of $1, received periodically for 8 periods, discounted at 7% is 5.9713.

$$\text{Periodic payment} = \frac{\text{Note Balance}}{5.9713}$$

$$\text{Periodic payment} = \frac{\$220,000}{5.9713} = \$36,843$$

Part 2

Period Ending	(a) Beginning Principal Balance	(b) Periodic Payment	(c) Interest Expense for the Period (a) × 7%	(d) Portion of Payment That is Principal (b) − (c)	(e) Ending Principal Balance (a) − (d)
Nov. 30/02	$220,000	$36,843	$15,400	$21,443	$198,557
Apr. 30/03	198,557	36,843	13,899	22,944	175,613
Nov. 30/03	175,613	36,843	12,293	24,550	151,063
Apr. 30/04	151,063	36,843	10,574	26,269	124,794
Nov. 30/04	124,794	36,843	8,736	28,107	96,687
Apr. 30/05	96,687	36,843	6,768	30,075	66,612
Nov. 30/05	66,612	36,843	4,663	32,180	34,432
Apr. 30/06	34,432	36,843	2,411*	34,432	0
Total....................		$294,744	$74,744	$220,000	

* *Adjusted for rounding.*

Fundamental Accounting Principles, Tenth Canadian Edition

Problem 17-10B (continued)

Part 3

2002				
Nov. 30	Interest Expense...		15,400	
	Notes Payable..		21,443	
	Cash...			36,843
Dec. 31	Interest Expense (13,899 × 1/6)		2,317	
	Interest Payable			2,317
2003				
Apr. 30	Interest Payable		2,317	
	Interest Expense (13,899 × 5/6)		11,582	
	Notes Payable..		22,944	
	Cash...			36,843

Part 4

Period Ending	(a) Beginning Balance	(b) Interest Expense	(c) Note Payable	(d) Cash	(e) Ending Balance
Nov. 30/02.........	$220,000	$ 15,400	$ 27,500	$ 42,900	$192,500
Apr. 30/03	192,500	13,475	27,500	40,975	165,000
Nov. 30/03.........	165,000	11,550	27,500	39,050	137,500
Apr. 30/04	137,500	9,625	27,500	37,125	110,000
Nov. 30/04.........	110,000	7,700	27,500	35,200	82,500
Apr. 30/05	82,500	5,775	27,500	33,275	55,000
Nov. 30/05.........	55,000	3,850	27,500	31,350	27,500
Apr. 30/06	27,500	1,925	27,500	29,425	0
Totals..............		$69,300	$220,000	$289,300	

2002				
Nov. 30	Interest Expense...		15,400	
	Notes Payable..		27,500	
	Cash...			42,900
	Principal included in each payment = $220,000/8			
	= $27,500			
Dec. 31	Interest Expense (13,475 × 1/6)		2,246	
	Interest Payable			2,246

*Problem 17-11B (80 minutes)

Part 1

The initial amount of the net liability is the present value of the six lease payments, discounted at 9%.

Part 2

Year	(a) Beginning Net Liability	(b) 9% Interest Expense	(c) Less Annual Payment	(d) Ending Net Liability
2001	$583,169	$ 52,485	$130,000	$505,654
2002	505,654	45,509	130,000	421,163
2003	421,163	37,905	130,000	329,068
2004	329,068	29,616	130,000	228,684
2005	228,684	20,582	130,000	119,266
2006	119,266	10,734	130,000	0
Total expense		$196,831		

Part 3

2001

Jan. 1	Machinery..	583,167	
	Lease Liability..		583,167
	To record signing of lease agreement.		

Part 4

2002

Dec. 31	Amortization Expense, Machinery	83,310	
	Accumulated Amort., Machinery		83,310
	($583,167/7)		

*Problem 17-11B *(continued)*

2002

Dec. 31	Lease liability	130,000	
	Cash...		130,000
	To record annual lease payment.		

Or, these two entries can be combined as follows:

Dec. 31	Interest Expense.......................................	45,509	
	Lease Liability	84,491	
	Cash...		130,000
	To record annual lease payment.		

Balance Sheet
December 31, 2002

Capital assets			
	Machinery	$583,169	
	Less: Accumulated amortization	166,620	$416,549
Long-term liabilities			
	Lease liability		$421,163

Part 5

2004

Jan. 4	Machinery	29,200	
	Cash...		29,200
	To record overhaul of machinery.		
Dec. 31	Amortization expense, machinery	51,777	
	Accumulated amortization, machinery...		51,777
	(accumulated amortization to date		
	$83,310 × 3 = $249,930)		
	(Book value after overhaul =		
	$583,169 + $29,200		
	less $249,930 = $362,439)		
	Revised amortization = $362,439/7 = $51,777		

*Problem 17-11B *(continued)*

Part 6

2007

Sept. 30	Amortization Expense, Machinery	38,833	
	Accumulated Amort., Machinery		38,833
	($51,777 × 9/12)		
30	Machinery	330,000	
	Accumulated amortization, machinery	444,094	
	Loss on exchange of machinery	103,273	
	Machinery		612,367
	Cash		265,000

(accumulated amortization at exchange =
$249,930 + (3 × $51,777) + 38,833 = $444,094)
(Book value at exchange =
* $612,367 – 444,094 = $168,273)*
(Loss on exchange =
* $168,273 – $65,000 = $103,273)*

Fundamental Accounting Principles, Tenth Canadian Edition

Chapter 18   Long-Term Investments and International Accounting

EXERCISES

Exercise 18-1 (30 minutes)

Mar. 21	Temporary investments	60,000	
	Cash...		60,000
	Purchased 90-day, 10% notes.		
Apr. 16	Temporary investments	51,750	
	Cash...		51,750
	Purchased 2,000 common shares.		
	Cost is (2,000 × $25.50) + $750.		
May 2	Temporary investments	40,000	
	Cash...		40,000
	Purchased 9% notes due May 2, 2003.		
June 20	Cash	61,479.45	
	Temporary Investments		60,000.00
	Interest Earned......................................		1,479.45
	Collected proceeds of 90-day note		
	Interest = 60,000 × 10% × 90/365.		
Sept. 21	Cash	2,000	
	Dividend Revenue..................................		2,000
	Received dividends on Windsor Motors		
	shares.		
Oct. 6	Cash	27,650	
	Temporary Investments		25,875
	Gain on Sale of Temporary Investments		1,775
	Sold 1,000 shares of Windsor Motors		
	Proceeds = (1,000 × $28) − $350.		
Nov. 2	Cash	1,800	
	Interest Revenue		1,800
	Received interest ($40,000 × .09 × 6/12).		

Exercise 18-3 (15 minutes)

	Cost	Market	LCM
Nortel common shares	$17,600	$19,450	
Northern Electric common shares	42,750	42,050	
Imperial Oil common shares	25,200	24,250	
Inco Limited common shares	34,800	31,950	
Total	$120,350	$117,700	$117,700

2001

Dec. 31 Loss on Market Decline of Temporary Investments 2,650

            Allowance to reduce Temporary

              Investments to Market 2,650

      ($120,350 – $117,700 = $2,650.)

Exercise 18-5

2002

Dec. 31 Loss on Market Decline of Temporary Investments 750

            Allowance to Reduce Temporary

              Investments to Market 750

        Allowance Dec. 31/01 = $23,500 – $22,000 = $1,500 credit

        Allowance Dec. 31/02 = $26,500 – $24,250 = $2,250 credit

        Loss for 2002 = $2,250 – $1,500 = $750.

Exercise 18-7 (20 minutes)

May 1	Investment in Hanna Company Bonds......................................	64,463	
	Interest Receivable	2,500	
	Cash..		66,963

To record purchase of Hanna Company bonds between
Interest dates.
(Purchase price = $75,000 × 85.95% + $1,000 = $64,463)
(Accrued interest = $75,000 × 10% × 4/12) = $2,500).

b.

June 30	Cash ($75,000 × .10 × 6/12)	3,750	
	Interest Receivable		2,500
	Interest Revenue ($75,000 × .10 × 2/12)		1,250

To record first interest receipt.

30	Investment in Hanna Company Bonds.......................................	1,157	
	Interest Revenue		1,157

To record amortization of Hanna Company Bonds
($64,463 × .125 × 2/12) = $1,343; $2,500 − 1,343 = $1,157.

Exercise 18-9 (15 minutes)

July 1	Investment in Margaree Company Bonds	38,293.60	
	Cash		38,293.60
	Purchased Margaree Company bonds.		

Dec. 31	Cash	1,000.00	
	Investment in Margaree Company	148.80	
	Bond Interest Revenue		1,148.80

To record interest earned at a market rate
($38,293.60 × .06 × 6/12 = $1,148.80 interest earned)
($40,000 × .05 × 6/12 = $1,000 cash received)
($1,148.80 – $1,000 = $148.80 amortization of bond discount).

Exercise 18-11 (30 minutes)

1999

Dec. 31	Unrealized Holding Loss	5,200	
	Long-Term Investments, ...		5,200

$170,000 – $164,800 = $5,200 loss.
This entry assumes the decline in market value below cost is non-temporary

2000

No entry

2001

No entry

2002

Dec. 31	Unrealized Holding Loss	44,000	
	Long-Term Investments		44,000

$398,000 – $354,000 = $44,000 loss.
This entry assumes the decline in market value below cost is non-temporary.

Exercise 18-13 (25 minutes)

Quarter ended June 30, 2002:

June 2 recorded amount (980,000 × $0.16720)	$ 163,856
June 30 balance sheet amount (980,000 × $0.17100)	167,580
Gain reported during quarter	$ 3,724

Quarter ended September 30, 2002:

June 30 balance sheet amount	$ 167,580
Sept. 30 balance sheet amount (980,000 × $0.17225)	168,805
Gain reported during quarter	$ 1,225

Quarter ended December 31, 2002:

Sept. 30 balance sheet amount	$ 168,805
Dec. 31 balance sheet amount (980,000 × $0.16885)	165,473
Loss reported during quarter	$ 3,332

Quarter ended March 31, 2003:

Dec. 31 balance sheet amount	$ 165,473
Jan. 3, 2003, amount received (980,000 × $0.17310)	169,638
Gain reported during quarter	$ 4,165

Note that the combined net gain for all four quarters equals $5,782 ($3,724 + $1,225 – $3,332 + $4,165).

This amount also equals the difference between the number of dollars finally received ($169,638) and the initial measure of the account receivable ($163,856).

And, this amount equals the number of francs (980,000) owed by the customer times the change ($0.00590) in the exchange rate between the beginning rate ($0.16720) and the ending rate ($0.17310).

PROBLEMS

Problem 18-1B

Feb.	5	Temporary Investments	105,757	
		Cash (3,500 × $29.50 + $2,507)		105,757
		Purchased shares of Westburne.		
	16	Temporary Investments	20,000	
		Cash		20,000
		Purchased treasury bills.		
Apr.	7	Temporary Investments	16,377	
		Cash (1,200 × $13.25) + $477)		16,377
		Purchased 1,200 shares of Gentra.		
June	2	Temporary Investments	84,740	
		Cash (2,500 × $32.75) + $2,865)		84,740
		Purchased 2,500 shares of Zycom.		
	30	Cash..	6,125	
		Dividends Earned (3,500 × $1.75).............................		6,125
		Received dividends on Sask shares.		
Aug.	11	Cash (875 × $25 − $531)	21,344	
		Loss on Sale of Temporary Investments	5,095	
		Temporary Investments		26,439
		Sold 875 shares of Sask.		
	17	Cash	20,500	
		Temporary Investments		20,000
		Interest Earned (5% × $20,000 × 6/12)......................		500
		Proceeds of treasury shares.		
	24	Cash (1,200 × $0.20)	240	
		Dividends Earned		240
		Received dividends from Gentra shares.		
Dec.	18	Cash (1,200 × $0.45)	540	
		Dividends Earned		540
		Received dividends on Gentra shares.		

Fundamental Accounting Principles, Tenth Canadian Edition

Problem 18-1B *(continued)*

Dec. 20 Cash (2,625 × $1)	2,625	
Dividends Earned		2,625
Received dividends from Sask shares (3,500 – 875).		

Problem 18-2B

Part 1

2002

Jan. 11 Temporary Investments	50,000	
Cash..		50,000
Purchased treasury bills.		
Feb. 2 Temporary Investments	23,330	
Cash (600 × $38.50 + $230)..........................		23,330
Purchased 600 common shares of Shell Canada.		
Feb. 13 Temporary Investments	19,700	
Cash (2,000 × $9.75) + $200.........................		19,700
Purchased 2,000 shares of Air Canada.		
Mar. 2 Temporary Investments	25,000	
Cash		25,000
Purchased Treasury notes due March 2, 2003.		
27 Temporary Investments	41,906	
Cash (1,200 × $34.63) + $350................................		41,906
Purchased 1,200 shares.		
June 8 Cash (600 × $0.35)	210	
Dividend Revenue		210
Received dividends on Shell shares.		
17 Cash (400 × $40) – $160	15,840.00	
Temporary Investments ($23,330 × 400/600)		15,553.33
Gain on sale of Temporary Investments.................		286.67
Sold 400 common shares of Shell Canada.		
July 13 Cash	52,005	
Temporary Investments..................................		50,000
Interest earned ($50,000 × .08 × 183/365)................		2,005

Proceeds of treasury bills that matured on July 11/02.

Aug. 12 Cash	200	
Dividend Revenue...		200
Received dividends on Air Canada shares.		
Sept. 2 Cash ($25,000 × 0.09 × 6/12)	1,125	
Interest Revenue...		1,125
Received interest on Treasury notes due September 2.		
8 Cash (200 × $0.35)	70	
Dividend Revenue...		70
Received dividends on Shell Canada shares.		
Nov. 12 Cash (2,000 × $0.25)	500	
Dividend Revenue...		500
Received dividends on Air Canada shares.		

Part 2

Temporary Equity Securities	Cost	Market	LCM
Shell Canada ($23,330 × 200/600)	$ 7,776.67		
200 × 40.13		$ 8,026.00	
Air Canada	19,700.00		
2,000 × $8.50		17,000.00	
Nortel	41,906.00		
1,200 × $34.00		40,800.00	
Totals	$69,382.67	$65,826.00	$65,825

Part 3

2002

Dec. 31 Interest Receivable	750.00	
Interest Revenue...		750.00
To accrue interest on Treasury notes		
($25,000 × .09 × 4/12).		
Dec. 31 Loss on decline of Temporary Investments...........................	3,556.67	
Allowance to Reduce Temporary		
Investments to Cost..		3,556.67
To adjust temporary investments portfolio		

To lower of LCM amount ($69,382.67 – $65,876.00).

Problem 18-3B *Part 1*

2002
Jan.   1 Investment in Foster Company Bonds 92,905
           Cash...   92,905
           To record investment.

June 30 Cash ($90,000 × 11% × 6/12) 4,950
           Investment in Foster Company Bonds   305
           Investment Revenue ($92,905 × .10 × 6/12).................   4,645
           To record six months' interest revenue and discount
           amortization.

2002
Dec. 31 Cash ($90,000 × 11% × 6/12) 4,950
           Investment in Foster Company Bonds   320
           Investment Revenue ($92,600 × .10 × 6/12).................   4,630
           To record six months' interest revenue and discount
           amortization ($92,905 – $305 = $92,600).

Problem 18-4B *Part 1*

1.   Equity securities on December 31, 2002:

Security	Cost Carrying	Market Value
Cost basis:		
45,000 common shares of Roe Company	$1,118,250	$1,136,250
12,750 common shares of Shore	462,570	200,750
85,000 common shares of Victor	272,250	269,875
10,000 common shares of Xplus	99,840	91,250
Total	$1,952,910	$1,698,125
Equity basis:		
31,000 common shares of Uris	$ 575,650	$ 545,600
5,000 common shares of Wong	103,100	109,375
Total	$ 678,750	$ 654,975

Problem 18-4B *(continued)*

Part 1

Long-term investment in Equity securities would be reported on the December 31, 2002 balance sheet at cost and the market values would be disclosed in brackets on the face of the statement or in the accompanying notes. Market values of Victor and Xplus shares are below cost but it is unlikely that an adjustment would be made unless it was reasonable to assume that the market declines were permanent. The share of Shore would be written down to market since the decrease is permanent:

Part 2

Dec. 31 Unrealized Loss Due to Market Decline	261,820	
Long-Term Investments		261,820

Part 3

2002 realized gain (loss):

	Cost	Market	Gain (loss)
4,250 shares of Shore Company...........................	$154,190	$142,110	$(12,080)
22,000 shares of Tate Company...........................	294,470	308,100	13,630
Realized gain (loss) for 2002................................			$ 1,550

Problem 18-5B (50 minutes) *Part 1*

1) 2001

Jan. 12	Investment in Turner Company	250,000	
	Cash		250,000
Mar. 31	Cash (12,000 × $1.00)	12,000	
	Investment in Turner Company		12,000
Dec. 31	Investment in Turner Company	30,000	
	Earnings from Investment in Turner Company ($125,000 × 24%)		30,000
2002			
Aug. 15	Cash (12,000 × $0.80)	9,600	
	Investment in Turner Company		9,600
Dec. 31	Earnings from Investment in Turner Company ($95,000 × 24%)	22,800	
	Investment Turner Company		22,800

Problem 18-5B *(continued)*

Part 1

```
2003
Jan.  6 Cash ..................................................................  230,000
         Loss on Sale of Investments .............................    5,600
            Investment in Trumpe Company ...........................              235,600
         ($250,000 – $12,000 + $30,000 – $9,600
         + $22,800 = $235,600).
```

2) Investment Cost per Share, January 1, 2003:
   $250,000 – $12,000 + $30,000 – $9,600 + $22,800 = $235,600
   $235,600/12,000 = $19.63

3) Retained Earnings of River Company, January 7, 2003:

Earnings from investment in Turner Company-2001	$30,000
Loss from investment in Turner Company-2002	(22,800)
Loss on sale of investments	(5,600)
Retained earnings, January 7, 2003	$ 1,600

Part 2

```
2001
Jan.  9 Investment in Turner Company ...............................  250,000
            Cash ..........................................................................              250,000


Apr. 30 Cash (12,000 × $1.00) ...........................................   12,000
            Dividends Earned ........................................................               12,000


2002
Aug. 10 Cash (12,000 × $0.80) ...........................................    9,600
            Dividends Earned ........................................................                9,600


2003
Jan.  6 Cash ..................................................................  230,000
         Loss on Sale of Investments....................................   20,000
            Investment in Turner Company ...................................              250,000
```

2) Investment Cost per Share, January 7, 2003:
   $250,000/10,000 = $25.00

Problem 18-5B (continued)

Part 2

3) Retained Earnings of River Company, January 7, 2003:

Dividends earned-2001	$12,000
Dividends earned-2002	9,600
Gain on sale of investments	(20,000)
Retained earnings, January 7, 2003	$ 1,600

Problem 18-6B (60 minutes) *Part 1*

2001

July 16	Accounts Receivable-Shisedu Company	7,502.15	
	Sales..		7,502.15
	(950,000 × $0.007897 = $7,502.15).		
Aug. 21	Cash	9,500.00	
	Sales..		9,500.00
Sept. 14	Cash (950,000 × $0.007779)	7,390.05	
	Foreign Exchange Gain or Loss............................	112.10	
	Accounts Receivable-Shisedu Company.................		7,502.15
Oct. 6	Accounts Receivable-Trafalgar Distributors...................	8,822.00	
	Sales		8,822.00
	(5,000 × $1.7644 = $8,822).		
Nov. 18	Accounts Receivable-Belique Suppliers	8,454.00	
	Sales..		8,454.00
	(30,000 × $0.2818 = $8,454).		
Dec. 31	Foreign Exchange Gain or Loss.....................................	112.00	
	Accounts Receivable-Trafalgar Distributors		112.00
	(5,000 × $1.7644) = $8,822.00		
	(5,000 × $1.7420) = 8,710.00		
	$ 112.00		
31	Accounts Receivable-Belgique Suppliers	96.00	
	Foreign Exchange Gain or Loss		96.00
	(30,000 × $0.2818) = $8,454.00		
	(30,000 × $0.2850) = 8,550.00		
	$ 96.00		

Problem 18-6B *(continued) Part 1*

2002

Jan.	4	Cash (5,000 × $1.7695)	8,847.50	
		Foreign Exchange Gain or Loss		137.50
		Accounts Receivable-Trafalgar Distributors...........		8,710.00
		($8,822.00 – $112.00 = $8,710.00).		

Problem 18-6B (60 minutes) *Part 1*

2002

Jan.	17	Cash (30,000 × $0.2822)	8,466	
		Foreign Exchange Gain or Loss	84	
		Accounts Receivable-Belgique Suppliers		8,550
		($8,454.00 + $96.00 = $8,550.00).		

Part 2

Exchange loss in 2001: $112.10 + $112.00 – $96.00 = $128.10

Analysis Component:

To reduce the risk of foreign exchange gain or loss, Paul Power could attempt to negotiate foreign customer sales that are denominated in Canadian dollars. To accomplish this, Paul Power may be willing to offer favourable terms, such as price discounts or longer credit terms. Another possibility that may be of limited potential is for Global Enterprises to make credit purchases denominated in foreign currencies, planning the purchases so that the payables in foreign currency match the foreign currency receivables in time and amount.

NOTE: A few students may also understand Global Enterprises' opportunity of hedging. This involves selling foreign currency futures to be delivered at the time the receivables from foreign customers will be collected.

*Problem 18-7B *Part 1*

Common shares, Smaller Company...	200,000	
Retained Earnings, Smaller Company	225,000	
Excess of Cost over book value...	49,500	
Investment in Smaller Company(20,000 × .9 × $24)	432,000	
Minority Interest ($200,000 + $225,000) × 10%)		42,500

The amount of retained earnings shown on the consolidated balance sheet equals the amount recorded in the parent company's account. The subsidiary's retained earnings is eliminated. Thus, on January 1, 2001, consolidated retained earnings is $350,500.

*Problem 18-7B (continued)

Part 2

Investment in Smaller Company, Jan. 1/01	$432,000.00
Plus: Earnings from investment (.9 × $45,000)	40,500.00
Less: Dividend received from Smaller (.9 × $25,000)	−22,500.00
Investment in Smaller Company, December 31, 2001.	$602,400.00
Retained Earnings, Larger Jan. 1/01	$350,500.00
Plus: Net income excluding investment income....................................	90,000.00
Earnings from investment in Smaller	40,500.00
Less: Dividend declared by Larger...	−45,000.00
Retained Earnings, Larger Company, December 31, 2001.	$436,000.00

LARGER COMPANY AND SMALLER COMPANY
Worksheet for Consolidated Balance Sheet
As of December 31, 2001

	Larger	Smaller	Eliminations Debit	Eliminations Credit	Consolidated
Cash	140,200	106,800			247,000
Notes receivable	45,000			a) 45,000	
Merchandise	220,800	175,300			396,100
Building-net	284,250	240,000			524,250
Land	186,000	183,500			369,500
Investment in Smaller	450,000			b) 450,000	
Excess of cost over book value			b) 49,500		49,500
	1,326,250	705,600			1,586,350
Accounts Payable	215,250	215,600			430,850
Note Payable		45,000	a) 45,000		
Common Shares, Larger	675,000				675,000
Retained Earnings, Larger	436,000				436,000
Common Shares, Smaller		200,000	b) 200,000		
Retained Earnings, Smaller		245,000	b) 245,000**		
Minority Interest				b) 44,500*	44,500
	1,326,250	705,600	539,500	539,500	1,586,350

* ($200,000 + $245,000) × 10% = $44,500
**$225,000 + $45,000 − $25,000 = $245,000

Chapter 19   Reporting and Analyzing Cash Flows

EXERCISES

Exercise 19-1 (15 minutes)

		Operating Activities	Investing Activities	Financing Activities	Noncash Investing & Financing Activities	Not Reported on Statement or in Footnote
		Statement of cash flows				
a.	Long-term bonds payable were retired by issuing common shares.				X	
b.	Surplus merchandise inventory was sold for cash.	X				
c.	Borrowed cash from the bank by signing a nine-month note payable.			X		
d.	Paid cash to purchase a patent.		X			
e.	A six-month note receivable was accepted in exchange for a building that had been used in operations.				X	
f.	Recorded amortization expense on all plant assets.	X				
g.	A cash dividend that had been declared in a previous period was paid in the current period.			X		

Exercise 19-3 (25 minutes)

Case A:

Sales revenue		$255,000
Accounts receivable, December 31	$17,400	
Accounts receivable, January 1	(12,600)	
Less increase in accounts receivable		4,800
Cash receipts from customers		$250,200

Case B:

Insurance expense		$ 34,200
Prepaid insurance, December 31..............................	$ 8,550	
Prepaid insurance, January 1	(5,700)	
Plus increase in prepaid insurance		2,850
Cash paid for insurance		$ 37,050

Exercise 19-3 (continued)

Case C:

Salaries expense		$102,000
Salaries payable, December 31...............................	$ 7,500	
Salaries payable, January 1	(6,300)	
Less increase in salaries payable		1,200
Cash paid for salaries.....................................		$100,800

Exercise 19-5 (30 minutes)

Cash flows from operating activities:

Receipts from customers (See note a)......................	$ 592,500
Payments for merchandise (See note b)	(310,500)
Payments for salaries (See note c)..........................	(84,345)
Payments for rent..	(16,200)
Payments for utilities....................................	(6,375)
Net cash provided by operating activities.................	$ 175,080

Note a: Sales – Increase in receivables

$606,000 – $13,500 = $592,500

Note b: Cost of goods sold + Increase in inventory + Decrease in payables

$297,000 + $9,000 + $4,500 = $310,500

Note c: Salaries expense + Decrease in salaries payable

$82,845 + $1,500 = $84,345

Fundamental Accounting Principles, Tenth Canadian Edition

Exercise 19-7 (20 minutes)

Part 1

Cash flows from operating activities:

Net income..	$ 90,000
Adjustments to reconcile net income to net cash provided by operating activities:	
Increase in accounts receivable...........................	(8,000)
Decrease in merchandise inventory	10,000
Increase in prepaid expenses.............................	(2,000)
Increase in accounts payable	7,000
Decrease in salaries payables	(4,000)
Amortization expense..	20,000
Net cash provided by operating activities	$113,000

Part 2

Cash flows from operations is different from net income because net income is based on accrual accounting which recognizes transactions (revenues and expenses) as they occur regardless of whether cash is received/paid. Cash flows from operations records revenues and expenses only when the respective cash is actually received/paid.

Exercise 19-9 (15 minutes)

		Statement of cash flows		Footnote Describing Noncash Investing & Financing Activities	Not Reported on Statement or in Footnote
	Operating Activities	Investing Activities	Financing Activities		
a. Land for a new capital asset was purchased by issuing common shares				X	
b. Recorded amortization expense	X				
c. Income taxes payable increased by 15% from prior year	X				
d. Declared and paid a cash dividend			X		
e. Paid cash to purchase merchandise					X
f. Sold capital equipment at a loss	X	X			
g. Accounts receivable decreased during the year	X				

Exercise 19-11

(1)
Sales	$655,000
Less increase in accounts receivable	(18,000)
Cash received from customers	$637,000

(2)
Cost of goods sold	$399,000
Less decrease in merchandise inventory	(30,000)
Purchases	369,000
Plus decrease in accounts payable	6,000
Cash paid for merchandise	$375,000

(3)
Other operating expenses	$ 67,000
Plus decrease in wages payable	9,000
Plus increase in prepaid expenses	200
Cash paid for other operating expenses	$ 76,200

(4)
Income taxes expense	$ 45,640
Plus decrease in income taxes payable	1,200
Cash paid for income taxes	$ 46,840

(5)
Cost of equipment sold	$ 48,600
Accumulated amortization of equipment sold	(40,600)
Book value of equipment sold	8,000
Gain on sale of equipment	2,000
Cash receipt from sale of equipment	$ 10,000

Cost of equipment sold	$ 48,600
Plus increase in the equipment account balance	10,000
Cash paid for new equipment	$ 58,600

Equipment				Accumulated Amortization, Equipment		
Balance, 30/6/2001	120,000				Balance, 30/6/2001	10,000
Purchase	58,600	Sale	48,600	Sale 40,600	Amort. expense	58,600
Balance, 30/6/2002	130,000				Balance, 30/6/2002	28,000

(6)
Carrying value of notes retired	30,000
Cash paid to retire notes	$30,000

Exercise 19-11 *(continued)*

(7) Net income $86,760
    Less increase in retained earnings   17,200
    Cash paid for dividends $69,560

CORMIER LTD.
Statement of cash flows (Direct Method)
For Year Ended June 30, 2002

Cash flows from operating activities:

Cash received from customers	$ 637,000	
Cash paid for merchandise	(375,000)	
Cash paid for other operating expenses	(76,200)	
Cash paid for income taxes	(46,840)	
Net cash provided by operating activities		$138,960

Cash flows from investing activities:

Cash received from sale of office equipment	$ 10,000	
Cash paid for store equipment	(58,600)	
Net cash used in investing activities		(48,600)

Cash flows from financing activities:

Cash received from issuance of common shares	50,000	
Cash paid to retire bonds payable	$ (30,000)	
Cash paid for dividends	(69,560)	
Net cash used in financing activities		(49,560)
Net increase in cash		$ 40,800
Cash balance at beginning of year		35,000
Cash balance at end of year		$ 75,800

Exercise 19-13

Adjustments to derive cash flow from operations:

	Adjust by	
	Adding	**Subtracting**
1. Changes in current assets:		
a. Increases		X
b. Decreases	X	
2. Changes in current liabilities:		
a. Increases	X	
b. Decreases		X
3. Amortization of capital assets	X	
4. Amortization of intangible assets	X	
5. Interest expense:		
a. Bond Premium amortized		X
b. Bond Discount amortized.................................	X	
6. Sale of noncurrent asset:		
a. Gain		X
b. Loss	X	

PROBLEMS

Problem 19-1B (35 minutes)

POLTACK COMPANY
Statement of Cash Flows
For Year Ended December 31, 2002

Cash flows from operating activities:

Cash received from customers (1)	$859,005	
Cash paid for merchandise (2)	(436,275)	
Cash paid for other operating expenses	(251,685)	
Cash paid for income taxes (3)	(65,940)	
Net cash provided by operating activities		$105,105
Cash flows from investing activities:		
Cash paid for equipment		(40,530)
Cash flows from financing activities:		
Cash received from issuing common		
shares (4,200 × $14)	$ 58,800	
Cash paid for dividends	(92,400)	
Net cash used by financing activities		(33,600)
Net increase in cash		$ 30,975
Cash balance at beginning of 2002		44,520
Cash balance at end of 2002		$ 75,495

Supporting calculations:

(1) Sales + Decrease in receivables

$853,650 + ($32,550 − $27,195) = $859,005

(2) Cost of   + Increase in − Increase in
goods sold   inventory   payables

$390,600 + ($245,490 − $195,825) − ($53,865 − $49,875) = $436,275

(3) Income taxes expense + Decrease in income taxes payable

$62,790 + ($9,450 − $6,300) = $65,940

Fundamental Accounting Principles, Tenth Canadian Edition

Problem 19-2B (35 minutes)

POLTACK COMPANY
Statement of Cash Flows
For Year Ended December 31, 2002

Cash flows from operating activities:		
Net income		$123,795
Adjustments to reconcile net income to net cash		
provided by operating activities:		
Decrease in accounts receivable ($32,550 – $27,195)	5,355	
Increase in merchandise inventory ($245,490 – $195,825) ...	(49,665)	
Increase in accounts payable ($53,865 – $49,875)	3,990	
Decrease in income taxes payable ($9,450 – $6,300)	(3,150)	
Amortization expense	24,780	
Net cash provided by operating activities		$105,105
Cash flows from investing activities:		
Cash paid for equipment		(40,530)
Cash flows from financing activities:		
Cash received from issuing common		
shares (4,200 × $14)	$58,800	
Cash paid for dividends	(92,400)	
Net cash used in financing activities		(33,600)
Net increase in cash		$30,975
Cash balance at beginning of 2002		44,520
Cash balance at end of 2002		$75,495

Problem 19-3B

Part 1

Cash dividends paid: $70,000 (Net income of $151,200 less $81,200 change in retained earnings)

Problem 19-3B *(continued)*

Part 2

FOTAN LTD.
Statement of Cash Flows
Year Ended December 31, 2002

Cash flows from operating activities:

Net income		$151,200
Add (deduct) changes to convert to cash basis:		
Accounts receivable	$(74,200)	
Inventory	(44,800)	
Accounts payable	(24,200)	
Amortization expense	60,200	
Loss on sale of equipment	5,600	
Gain on sale of long-term investment	(16,800)	(94,200)
Cash provided by operating activities		57,000
Cash flows from investing activities:		
Proceeds from sale of long-term investment	42,000	
Proceeds from sale of equipment	9,800	
Purchase of equipment	(28,000)	
Cash provided by investing activities		23,800
Cash flows from financing activities:		
Issuance of bonds payable	35,000	
Payment of dividend	(71,000)	
Cash used by financing activities		(36,000)
Increase in cash and temporary investments		44,800
Cash and temporary investments, January 1, 2002		50,400
Cash and temporary investments, December 2002		$ 95,200

Fundamental Accounting Principles, Tenth Canadian Edition

Problem 19-4B (50 minutes) *Part 1*

WOLFSON LIMITED
Statement of Cash Flows
For Year Ended December 31, 2002

Cash flows from operating activities:
Cash received from customers (1) $1,539,510
Cash paid for merchandise (2) .... (777,420)
Cash paid for other expenses (3) .... (547,050)
Cash paid for income taxes .... (13,230)
Net cash provided by operating activities...................... $201,810

Cash flows from investing activities:
Cash received from sale of equipment........................... $ 39,270
Cash paid for equipment (note A). .... (53,550)
Net cash used in investing activities .... (14,280)

Cash flows from financing activities:
Cash borrowed on short-term note .... $ 8,400
Cash paid on long-term note.. (63,000)
Cash received from issuing shares (4,200 × $11) 46,200
Cash paid for dividends .... (88,200)
Net cash provided by financing activities .... (96,600)
Net increase in cash .... $ 90,930
Cash balance at beginning of year................................. 100,170
Cash balance at end of year... $191,100

Note disclosure:
Note A

The company purchased equipment for $158,550 by signing a $105,000 long-term note payable and paying $53,550 in cash.

Supporting calculations:

(1) Sales + Decrease in receivables

$1,516,200 + ($127,050 − $103,740) = $1,539,510

(2) Cost of   − Decrease in + Decrease in
    goods sold   inventory   payables

$819,000 − ($686,280 − $636,300) + ($172,830 − $164,430) = $777,420

(3) Other expenses − Decrease in prepaid expenses

$549,990 − ($26,880 − $23,940) = $547,050

Problem 19-5B (40 minutes)

WOLFSON LIMITED
Statement of Cash Flows
For Year Ended December 31, 2002

Cash flows from operating activities:		
Net income	$79,800	
Adjustment to reconcile net income to net cash provided by operating activities:		
Decrease in accts. receivable ($127,050 – $103,740)	23,310	
Decrease in merchandise inv. ($686,280 – $636,300)	49,980	
Decrease in prepaid expenses ($26,880 – $23,940)	2,940	
Decrease in accounts payable ($172,830 – $164,430)......	(8,400)	
Amortization expense	51,240	
Loss on disposal of equipment	2,940	
Net cash provided by operating activities		$201,810
Cash flows from investing activities:		
Cash received from sale of equipment	$39,270	
Cash paid for equipment (note A)	(53,550)	
Net cash used in investing activities.................................		(14,280)
Cash flows from financing activities:		
Cash borrowed on short-term note....................................	$ 8,400	
Cash paid on long-term note...	(63,000)	
Cash received from issuing shares (4,200 × $11)	46,200	
Cash paid for dividends..	(88,200)	
Net cash provided by financing activities...........................		(96,600)
Net increase in cash..		$ 90,930
Cash balance at beginning of year		100,170
Cash balance at end of year...		$191,100

Note A

The company purchased equipment for $158,550 by signing a $105,000 long-term note payable and paying $53,550 in cash.

Fundamental Accounting Principles, Tenth Canadian Edition

*Problem 19-6B (50 minutes)

POLTACK COMPANY
Spreadsheet for Statement of Cash Flows
For Year Ended December 31, 2002

	December 31, 2001	Analysis of Changes		December 31, 2002
		Debit	Credit	
Balance sheet—debits:				
Cash...	44,520			75,495
Accounts receivable	32,550		(b) 5,355	27,195
Merchandise inventory...................	195,825	(c) 49,665		245,490
Equipment	107,100	(g) 40,530		147,630
	379,995			495,810
Balance sheet—credits:				
Accumulated Amort.,equipment....	42,840		(f) 24,780	67,620
Accounts payable...........................	49,875		(d) 3,990	53,865
Income taxes payable	9,450	(e) 3,150		6,300
Common shares	231,000		(h) 58,800	289,800
Retained earnings	46,830	(i) 92,400	(a) 123,795	78,225
	379,995			495,810
Statement of cash flows:				
Operating activities:				
Net income		(a) 123,795		
Decrease in accts. receivable		(b) 5,355		
Increase in merchandise inventory			(c) 49,665	
Increase in accounts payable		(d) 3,990		
Decrease in income taxes payable			(e) 3,150	
Amortization expense		(f) 24,780		
Investing activities:				
Payment for equipment			(g) 40,530	
Financing activities:				
Issued common shares for cash ...		(h) 8,800		
Paid cash dividends........................			(i) 92,400	
		402,465	402,465	

*Problem 19-7B (60 minutes)

WOLFSON LIMITED
Spreadsheet for Statement of cash flows
For Year Ended December 31, 2002

	December 31, 2001	Analysis of Changes Debit	Analysis of Changes Credit	December 31, 2002
Balance sheet—debits:				
Cash	100,170			191,100
Accounts receivable..........................	127,050		(b) 23,310	103,740
Merchandise inventory	686,280		(c) 49,980	636,300
Prepaid expenses	26,880		(d) 2,940	23,940
Equipment.......................................	302,400	(h) 158,550	(g) 71,400	389,550
	1,242,780			1,344,630
Balance sheet—credits:				
Accumulated amort, equipment.......	130,200	(g) 29,190	(f) 51,240	152,250
Accounts payable............................	172,830	(e) 8,400		164,430
Short-term notes payable	15,750		(j) 8,400	24,150
Long-term notes payable.................	115,500	(k) 63,000	(i) 105,000	157,500
Common shares................................	630,000		(l) 46,200	676,200
Retained earnings...........................	178,500	(m) 88,200	(a) 79,800	170,100
	1,242,780			1,344,630
Statement of cash flows:				
Operating activities:				
Net income		(a) 79,800		
Decrease in accts. receivable...........		(b) 23,310		
Decrease in merchandise inv.		(c) 49,980		
Decrease in prepaid expenses		(d) 2,940		
Decrease in accounts payable			(e) 8,400	
Amortization expense		(f) 51,240		
Loss on sale of equipment		(g) 2,940		
Investing activities:				
Receipts from sale of equipment......................................		(g) 39,270		
Payment to purchase equipment.....			(h) 53,550	
Financing activities:				
Borrowed on short-term note...........		(j) 8,400		
Payment on long-term note..............			(k) 63,000	
Issued common shares for cash......		(l) 46,200		
Payments of cash dividends			(m) 88,200	
Noncash investing and financing Activities (disclosed in note)				
Purchases of equipment financed by long-term note payable..............		(i) 105,000	(h) 105,000	
		756,420	756,420	

Fundamental Accounting Principles, Tenth Canadian Edition

Chapter 20   Analyzing Financial Statements

EXERCISES

Exercise 20-1 (20 minutes)

	2004	2003	2002	2001	2000
Sales	125	120	112	104	100
Cost of goods sold..............	127	121	114	105	100
Accounts receivable	127	122	116	108	100

The trend in sales is positive. While this is better than no growth, one cannot definitively say whether the sales trend is favourable without additional information about the economic conditions in which this trend occurred. Given the trend in sales, the comparative trends in cost of goods sold and accounts receivable both appear to be unfavourable. Both are increasing at faster rates than sales.

Exercise 20-3 (25 minutes)

	2002	2001
Sales	100.0%	100.0%
Cost of goods sold.......................	60.0	52.0
Gross profit from sales...............	40.0	48.0
Operating expenses....................	22.5	20.2
Net income................................	17.5%	27.8%

This situation appears to be unfavourable. Both cost of goods sold and operating expenses are taking a larger percent of each sales dollar in year 2002 compared to the prior year. Also, even though sales volume increased, net income decreased in absolute terms and dropped to only 17.5% of sales as compared to 27.8% in the year before.

Exercise 20-5 (25 minutes)

a. Current ratio:

2002: $$\frac{\$51,800 + \$186,800 + \$223,000 + \$19,400}{\$157,800} = \underline{1.87 \text{ to } 1}$$

2001: $$\frac{\$70,310 + \$125,940 + \$165,000 + \$18,750}{\$150,500} = \underline{2.52 \text{ to } 1}$$

2000: $$\frac{\$73,600 + \$98,400 + \$106,000 + \$8,000}{\$98,500} = \underline{2.90 \text{ to } 1}$$

b. Acid-test ratio:

2002: $$\frac{\$51,800 + \$186,800}{\$257,800} = \underline{0.93 \text{ to } 1}$$

2001: $$\frac{\$70,310 + \$125,940}{\$150,000} = \underline{1.30 \text{ to } 1}$$

2000: $$\frac{\$73,600 + \$98,400}{\$98,500} = \underline{1.75 \text{ to } 1}$$

Interpretation: Carmon's short-term liquidity position has weakened over the two-year period. Both the current and acid-test ratios show this declining trend. Although we do not have information about the nature of the company's business, the acid-test shift from 1.75 to 1 down to .93 to 1 and the current ratio shift from 2.90 to 1 down to 1.87 to 1 indicate a potential liquidity problem.

Exercise 20-7 (25 minutes)

a. Days' sales uncollected:

2002: $$\frac{\$186,800}{\$1,345,000} \times 365 = 51 \text{ days}$$

2001: $$\frac{\$125,940}{\$1,060,000} \times 365 = 44 \text{ days}$$

Fundamental Accounting Principles, Tenth Canadian Edition

Exercise 20-7 *(continued)*

b. Accounts receivable turnover:

2002: $$\frac{\$1,345,000}{(\$186,800 + \$125,940)/2} = 8.6 \text{ times}$$

2001: $$\frac{\$1,060,000}{(\$125,940 + \$98,400)/2} = 9.5 \text{ times}$$

c. Merchandise turnover:

2002: $$\frac{\$820,450}{(\$223,000 + \$165,000)/2} = 4.2 \text{ times}$$

2001: $$\frac{\$689,000}{(\$165,000 + \$106,000)/2} = 5.1 \text{ times}$$

d. Days' sales in inventory:

2002: $$\frac{\$223,000}{\$820,450} \times 365 = 99 \text{ days}$$

2001: $$\frac{\$165,000}{\$689,000} \times 365 = 87 \text{ days}$$

The number of days' sales uncollected has increased and the accounts receivable turnover has declined. The merchandise turnover has decreased and days' sales in inventory has increased. Although none of the changes that occurred from 2001 to 2002 appears to be dramatic, it may be true that Carmon is becoming less efficient in managing its inventory and collecting its receivables.

Exercise 20-9

Accounts Receivable Turnover:

Tate:
December 31, 2002

$$\frac{\$282,599}{(\$82,184 + \$53,081)/2} = 4.18 \text{ times}$$

Young:
December 31, 2002

$$\frac{\$137,984}{(\$78,448 + \$69,055)/2} = 1.87 \text{ times}$$

2. Tate   365 days/ 4.18 times turned = 87.32 days
    Young 365 days/1.87 times turned = 195.19 days

3. Tate is more efficient at collecting accounts receivable as it takes 87.32 days on average to collect an accounts receivable while it takes Young 195.19 days to collect on average.

                              Fundamental Accounting Principles, Tenth Canadian Edition

Exercise 20-11

Inventory turnovers:

	2002	2001
CGS/ average inventory		
Cost of goods sold......................	$310,000	$290,000
Average inventory:		
($52,000 +$44,000) ÷ 2	$ 48,000	
($44,000 + $38,000) ÷ 2		$ 41,000
Inventory turnover	<u>6.5</u>	<u>7.1</u>

The company's inventory turnover has decreased by 8.5%. If this is the beginning of a downward trend then it could be serious. However, a slowdown in inventory turnover is not bad if the company can achieve higher profits as a consequence of keeping more inventory on hand. Not enough information is given to reach a conclusion. Other things being equal, however, a decrease in inventory turnover is not good.

Exercise 20-13

$$\text{Total asset turnover for 2001} = \frac{\$2,431,000}{(\$793,000 + \$850,000)/2} = 2.96$$

$$\text{Total asset turnover for 2002} = \frac{\$3,771,000}{(\$850,000 + \$941,000)/2} = 4.21$$

Based on these calculations, Godoto turned its assets over 1.25 (4.21 – 2.96) more times in 2002 than in 2001. This increase indicates that Godoto became more efficient in using its assets. However, to evaluate Godoto's overall efficiency in using its assets, we would need to compare its turnover to that of other similar businesses.

Exercise 20-15

a. Debt and equity ratios:

	2002		2001	
Total liabilities (and debt ratio):				
$257,800 + $195,000.....................	$ 452,800	43.7%		
$150,500 + $205,000.....................			$355,500	39.9%
Total equity (and equity ratio):				
$325,000 + $258,200.....................	583,200	56.3		
$325,000 + $209,500.....................			534,500	60.1
Total liabilities and equity..............	$1,036,000	100.0%	$890,000	100.0%

b. Pledged assets to secured liabilities:

2002: $555,000/$195,000 = 2.85 to 1

2001: $510,000/$205,000 = 2.49 to 1

c. Times interest earned:

2002: ($68,200 + $17,050 + $22,200)/$22,200 = 4.84 times

2001: ($62,750 + $15,690 + $24,600)/$24,600 = 4.19 times

Interpretation: Carmon added debt to its capital structure during 2002, with the result that the debt ratio increased from 39.9% to 43.7%. However, the book value of pledged assets is well above secured liabilities (2.85 to 1 in 2002 and 2.49 to 1 in 2001), and the increased profitability of the company allowed it to increase the times interest earned from 4.19 to 4.84 times. Apparently, the company is able to handle the increased debt. However, we should note that the debt increase is entirely in current liabilities, which places a greater stress on short-term liquidity.

Exercise 20-17

Return on total assets = (Net income/Average total assets) × 100

2001: $36,400/[($320,000 + $750,000)/2] = .0680 × 100 = 6.8%

2002: $28,200/[($190,000 + $320,000)/2] = .1106 × 100 = 11.1%

Comment: Rawhide used its assets more efficiently in generating income in 2002 over 2001.

Exercise 20-19 (25 minutes)

Answer: The net income decreased.

Supporting calculations: When the sums of each year's common-size cost of goods sold and expenses are subtracted from the common-size sales percents, net income percents are as follows:

2000: 100.0 – 60.2 – 16.2 = 23.6% of sales
2001: 100.0 – 63.0 – 15.9 = 21.1% of sales
2002: 100.0 – 64.5 – 16.4 = 19.1% of sales

This means, for example, if 2000 sales are assumed to be $100, then sales for 2001 are $105.30 and the sales for 2002 are $106.50. If the income percents for the years are applied to these amounts, the net incomes are:

2000: $100.00 × 23.6% = $23.60
2001: $105.30 × 21.1% = $22.22
2002: $106.50 × 19.1% = $20.34

This shows that the company's net income decreased over the three years.

PROBLEMS

Problem 20-1B (60 minutes)

Part 1

Current ratios:
December 31, 2002: $226,000/$110,000 = <u>2.05 to 1</u>

December 31, 2001: $125,000/$92,000 = <u>1.36 to 1</u>

December 31, 2000: $179,000/$77,000 = <u>2.32 to 1</u>

Part 2

DEXTER CORPORATION
Common-Size Comparative Income Statement
For Years Ended December 31, 2002, 2001, and 2000

	2002	2001	2000
Sales	100.00%	100.00%	100.00%
Cost of goods sold	55.61	52.55	47.61
Gross profit	44.39	47.45	52.39
Selling expenses	13.37	12.56	15.35
Administrative expenses	10.00	12.68	13.38
Total expenses	23.37	25.24	28.73
Income before taxes	21.02	22.21	23.66
Income taxes	7.36	7.77	8.28
Net income	13.66	14.44	15.38

Part 3

DEXTER CORPORATION
Balance Sheet Data in Trend Percentages
For Years Ended December 31, 2002, 2001, and 2000

	2002	2001	2000
Assets			
Current assets	126.26	69.83	100.00%
Long-term investments	0.00	25.93	100.00
Plant and equipment	130.10	135.20	100.00
Total assets	123.08	110.70	100.00
Liabilities and Shareholders' Equity			
Current liabilities	142.86	119.48	100.00
Common Shares	122.50	122.50	100.00
Other contributed capital	119.11	103.60	100.00
Retained earnings	137.40	112.09	100.00
Total liabilities and equity	123.08	110.70	100.00

Fundamental Accounting Principles, Tenth Canadian Edition

Problem 20-1B *(continued)*

Part 4

Dexter's cost of goods sold took a larger percent of sales each year. Selling and administrative expenses and income taxes took a somewhat smaller portion each year, but not enough to offset the effect of cost of goods sold. As a result, income became a smaller percent of sales each year.

The large expansion of plant and equipment in 2001 was financed by a reduction in current assets, an increase in current liabilities, a large reduction in long-term investments, and apparently by a shares sale. One effect of this plan was to reduce the current ratio. However, the current ratio recovered in 2002. This apparently resulted from profits, limiting the amount of dividends paid, and the liquidation of long-term investments.

Problem 20-2B (120 minutes)

Part 1

	DOVER COMPANY Income Statement Trends For Years Ended December 31, 2005-1999						
	2005	2004	2003	2002	2001	2000	1999
Sales	80.4	83.9	82.1	87.5	94.6	92.9	100.0
Cost of goods sold...............	88.8	92.1	90.7	97.2	102.3	99.1	100.0
Operating expenses	78.4	81.2	80.4	87.8	90.6	92.2	100.0
Income before taxes..............	65.9	72.5	67.0	63.7	87.9	80.2	100.0

Problem 20-2B *(continued)*

<table>
<tr><th colspan="8" align="center">DOVER COMPANY
Balance Sheet Trends
December 31, 2005-1999</th></tr>
<tr><th></th><th>2005</th><th>2004</th><th>2003</th><th>2002</th><th>2001</th><th>2000</th><th>1999</th></tr>
<tr><td>Cash ....</td><td>65.2</td><td>71.7</td><td>69.6</td><td>78.3</td><td>97.8</td><td>91.3</td><td>100.0</td></tr>
<tr><td>Accounts receivable, net .....</td><td>78.0</td><td>87.3</td><td>83.9</td><td>85.6</td><td>94.9</td><td>93.2</td><td>100.0</td></tr>
<tr><td>Merchandise inventory ....</td><td>88.3</td><td>92.0</td><td>90.7</td><td>96.3</td><td>98.1</td><td>104.3</td><td>100.0</td></tr>
<tr><td>Other current assets ....</td><td>71.4</td><td>75.0</td><td>78.6</td><td>85.7</td><td>82.1</td><td>92.9</td><td>100.0</td></tr>
<tr><td>Long-term investments........</td><td>88.9</td><td>66.7</td><td>44.4</td><td>96.7</td><td>96.7</td><td>96.7</td><td>100.0</td></tr>
<tr><td>Plant and equip., net............</td><td>119.9</td><td>121.9</td><td>123.2</td><td>95.0</td><td>96.7</td><td>98.3</td><td>100.0</td></tr>
<tr><td>Total assets ....</td><td>97.5</td><td>98.4</td><td>95.4</td><td>92.6</td><td>96.2</td><td>98.0</td><td>100.0</td></tr>
<tr><td></td><td></td><td></td><td></td><td></td><td></td><td></td><td></td></tr>
<tr><td>Current liabilities ....</td><td>75.0</td><td>78.2</td><td>70.4</td><td>56.0</td><td>66.2</td><td>79.2</td><td>100.0</td></tr>
<tr><td>Long-term liabilities..............</td><td>59.1</td><td>65.9</td><td>72.7</td><td>79.5</td><td>86.4</td><td>93.2</td><td>100.0</td></tr>
<tr><td>Common Shares ....</td><td>100.0</td><td>100.0</td><td>100.0</td><td>100.0</td><td>100.0</td><td>100.0</td><td>100.0</td></tr>
<tr><td>Retained earnings.................</td><td>219.0</td><td>204.8</td><td>185.7</td><td>181.0</td><td>171.4</td><td>142.9</td><td>100.0</td></tr>
<tr><td>Total liabilities and
   Equity.................................</td><td>97.5</td><td>98.4</td><td>95.4</td><td>92.6</td><td>96.2</td><td>98.0</td><td>100.0</td></tr>
</table>

Part 2

The statements and the trend percent data show that sales declined every year. However, cost of goods sold did not fall as rapidly as sales. As a result, gross profit fell more rapidly than sales. Operating expenses fell less rapidly than gross profit. Manage-ment was not able to reduce costs and expenses fast enough to keep up with the sales decline.

Although the profits decreased during these years, the company did continue to earn a net income. It appears that the cash generated from operations was used primarily to reduce both current and long-term liabilities. In addition, the company made a large expansion of its plant and equipment during 2003, financing this expansion primarily through the liquidation of long-term investments.

Problem 20-3B (50 minutes)

a. Current ratio:

$$\frac{\$18{,}000 + \$14{,}700 + \$55{,}800 + \$6{,}200 + \$62{,}300 + \$2{,}800}{\$32{,}600 + \$4{,}200 + \$4{,}800} = \underline{3.84 \text{ to } 1}$$

b. Acid-test ratio:

$$\frac{\$18{,}000 + \$14{,}700 + \$55{,}800 + \$6{,}200}{\$32{,}600 + \$4{,}200 + \$4{,}800} = \underline{2.28 \text{ to } 1}$$

c. Days' sales uncollected:

$$\frac{\$55{,}800 + \$6{,}200}{\$697{,}200} \times 365 = \underline{32.5 \text{ days}}$$

d. Merchandise turnover:

$$\frac{\$458{,}300}{(\$64{,}800 + \$62{,}300)/2} = \underline{7.2 \text{ times}}$$

e. Days' sales in inventory:

$$\frac{\$62{,}300}{\$458{,}300} \times 365 = \underline{49.6 \text{ days}}$$

f. Ratio of pledged assets to secured liabilities:

$$\$306{,}300/\$125{,}000 = \underline{2.45 \text{ to } 1}$$

g. Times interest earned:

$$\$116{,}200/\$7{,}100 = \underline{16.4 \text{ times}}$$

h. Profit margin:

$$\frac{\$91{,}300 \times 100}{\$697{,}200} = \underline{13.1\%}$$

i. Total asset turnover:

$$\frac{\$697{,}200}{(\$466{,}100 + \$367{,}500)/2} = \underline{1.7 \text{ times}}$$

Problem 20-3B *(continued)*

j. Return on total assets:

$$\frac{\$91,300}{(\$466,100 + \$367,500)/2} \times 100 = \underline{21.9\%}$$

k. Return on common Shareholders' equity:

$$\frac{\$91,300}{(\$299,500 + \$266,700)/2} \times 100 = \underline{32.3\%}$$

Problem 20-4B (60 minutes)

Trans-action	Current Assets	Quick Assets	Current Liabilities	Current Ratio	Acid-Test Ratio	Working Capital
Beginning* Mar. 3	$ 286,000 + 55,000 − 36,000	$ 117,000 + 55,000	$ 130,000	2.2 to 1	0.9 to 1	$156,000
Bal. Mar. 5	$ 305,000 + 35,000 − 35,000	$ 172,000 + 35,000 − 35,000	$ 130,000	2.35:1	1.32:1	175,000
Bal. Mar. 10	$ 305,000 + 56,000	$ 172,000	$ 130,000 + 56,000	2.35 :1	1.32:1	175,000
Bal. Mar. 12	$ 361,000 + 60,000	$ 172,000 + 60,000	$ 186,000 + 60,000	1.94:1 1	0.92:1	175,000
Bal. Mar. 15	$ 421,000 + 90,000	$ 232,000 + 90,000	$ 246,000	1.71:1 1	0.94:1	175,000
Bal. Mar. 22	$ 511,000 −150,000	$ 322,000 −150,000	$ 246,000	2.08:1	1.31:1	265,000
Bal. Mar. 24	$ 361,000	$ 172,000	$ 246,000 + 70,000	1.47:1	0.70:1	115,000
Bal. Mar. 26	$ 361,000 −	$ 172,000 −	$ 316,000	1.14:1	0.54:1	45,000
Bal. Mar. 28	$ 361,000 − 45,000	$ 172,000 − 45,000	$ 316,000 − 45,000	1.14:1	0.54:1	45,000
Bal. Mar 30	$ 316,000 − 70,000	$ 127,000 −70,000	$ 271,000 − 70,000	1.17:1	0.47:1	45,000
Bal.	$ 246,000	$ 57,000	$ 201,000	1.22:1	0.28:1	45,000

*Beginning balances:

Current assets (given)	$286,000
Current liabilities ($286,000/2.20)........................	$130,000
Quick assets ($130,000 × 0.90)............................	$117,000

Fundamental Accounting Principles, Tenth Canadian Edition

Problem 20-5B (50 minutes)

1. No. The current ratio has improved but the acid-test ratio has been declining. Also, the accounts receivable and inventory are turning over more slowly. These conditions indicate that an increasing portion of current assets consists of accounts receivable and inventories from which debts cannot be paid.

2. No, the company is collecting debts more slowly as indicated by the slower accounts receivable turnover.

3. No. Sales are increasing and accounts receivable are turning over more slowly. Either of these trends would produce an increase in accounts receivable, even if the other remained unchanged.

4. Probably yes. Since there is nothing to indicate the contrary, cost of goods sold is probably increasing in proportion to sales. Consequently, with sales increasing, cost of goods sold increasing in proportion, and merchandise turning more slowly, the amount of investment in the inventory must be increasing.

5. Yes. If sales were assumed to have been $100 in 2000, the sales trend shows that they would be $124 in 2001 and $136 in 2002. Then, dividing each sales figure by its ratio of sales to capital assets would give $28.57 for capital assets (100/3.5) in 2000; $32.63 ($124/3.8) in 2001; and $33.17 ($136/4.1) in 2002.

6. No. The percentage of return on shareholders' equity declined from 12.75% to 10.5%.

7. The ratio of sales to capital assets increased from 3.5 in 2000 to 4.1 in 2002. However, the return on total assets fell from 11.8% in 2000 to 9.9% in 2002. Whether these results are derived from a more efficient use of assets depends on a comparison with other companies and on the expectations of the individual doing the evaluation.

8. The dollar amount of selling expense increased in 2001 and decreased sharply in 2002. Assuming sales figures of $100 in 2000, $124 in 2001 and $136 in 2002, and multiplying each by its ratio of selling expense to net sales ratio gives $16.80 of selling expenses in 2000. In 2001, selling expenses were $19.71 in 2001 and $13.87 in 2002.

Problem 20-6B

Evans's profit margins are consistently higher than Bower's. However, Bower has significantly higher total asset turnovers. As a result, Bower generates a substantially higher return on total assets.

The trends of both companies include growth in sales, total asset turnover, and return on total assets. However, Evans's rates of improvement are better than Bower's. These differences may result from the fact that Evans is only three years old while Bower is an older, more established company. Evans's operation is considerably smaller than Bower's, but that will not persist many more years if both companies continue to grow at their historical rates.

Problem 20-6B *(continued)*

To some extent, Bower's higher total asset turnovers may result from the fact that its assets may have been purchased years earlier. If the turnover calculations had been based on current values, the differences might be less striking. The relative ages of the assets may explain some of the difference in profit margins. Assuming Evans's assets are newer, they may require smaller maintenance expenses.

Bower successfully employed financial leverage in 2003. Its return on total assets was 9.2% compared to the 7% interest rate it paid to obtain assets from creditors. In contrast, Evans's return was only 6.1% as compared to the 7% interest rate.

Fundamental Accounting Principles, Tenth Canadian Edition

Appendix IV   Present and Future Values

EXERCISES

Exercise IV-1 (10 minutes)

a. (1)   Present Value of a single amount.
   (2)   Multiply p from Table IV.1 by $10,000.
   (3)   Use Table IV.1, Periods = 8, and Interest rate = 4%.
   "OR"
   (1)   Future Value of a single amount.
   (2)   Divide $10,000 by f from Table IV.2.
   (3)   Use Table IV.2, Periods = 8, and Interest rate = 4%.

b. (1)   Future Value of an Annuity.
   (2)   Divide $10,000 by f from Table IV.4.
   (3)   Use Table IV.4, Periods = 8, and Interest Rate = 4%.
   "OR"
   (1)   Present Value of an Annuity.
   (2)   Multiply p from Table IV.1 by $10,000 *and* divide by p from Table IV.3.
   (3)   Use Tables IV.1 *and* IV.3, Periods = 8, and Interest = 4%.

c. (1)   Future Value of an Annuity.
   (2)   Multiply $4,000 by f from Table IV.4.
   (3)   Use Table IV.4, Periods = 40, and Interest = 8%.
      Yes, you will have more than $1,000,000 in 4 years.

d. (1)   Present Value of an Annuity.
   (2)   Multiply $30,000 by f from Table IV.3.
   (3)   Use Table IV.3, Periods = 20, and Interest 10%.
[*Note: Students must recognize the present value of $225,000 received today is $225,000.*]
      The $30,000 annuity may have a higher present value, but you could choose to invest the $225,000 and earn more interest.

Exercise IV-3 (10 minutes)

In Table IV.2, where $n = 25$ and $f = 10.8347$, then $i = \underline{10\%}$.

Exercise IV-5 (10 minutes)

In Table IV.3, where $i = 10\%$ and $p = 8.2014$, then $n = \underline{18}$.

Exercise IV-7 (10 minutes)

In Table IV.4, where $i = 8\%$ and $f = 30.3243$, then $n = \underline{16}$.

Exercise IV-9 (15 minutes)

10 years × 4 quarters = 40 interest periods
8%/4 = 2% per quarter
In Table IV.2, where $n = 40$ and $i = 2\%$, then $f = 2.2080$.
Total accumulation = 2.2080 × $7,200 = $\underline{\$15,897.60}$

Exercise IV-11 (15 minutes)

$500,000 × 10% × 1/2 = $25,000 semiannual interest payment.
In Table IV.1, where $n = 30$ and $i = 4\%$, then $p = 0.3083$.
In Table IV.3, where $n = 30$ and $i = 4\%$, then $p = 17.2920$.

0.3083 × $500,000 =	$154,150	present value of maturity amount
17.2920 × $25,000 =	432,300	present value of interest payments
	$586,450	cash proceeds

Exercise IV-13 (15 minutes)

In Table IV.1, where $n = 6$ and $i = 10\%$, then $p = 0.5645$.
Present value of investment = $606,773 × 0.5645 = $\underline{\$342,523}$

Exercise IV-15 (15 minutes)

a. $90,000 × 0.6651 (using Table IV.1, $i = 6\%$, $n = 7$) = $\underline{\$59,859}$.

b. $20,000 × 2.4869 (using Table IV.3, $i = 10\%$, $n = 3$) = $\underline{\$49,738}$.

Fundamental Accounting Principles, Tenth Canadian Edition

Exercise IV-17 (10 minutes)

	Single Future Payment	Number of Years	Interest Rate	Table IV.1 Value	Amount Borrowed
a.	$40,000	3	4%	0.8890	$35,560
b.	75,000	7	8	0.5835	43,763
c.	52,000	9	10	0.4241	22,053
d.	18,000	2	4	0.9246	16,643
e.	63,000	8	6	0.6274	39,526
f.	89,000	5	2	0.9057	80,607

Exercise IV-19 (30 minutes)

a. Present value of the annuity:
   Payment size $13,000
   Number of payments 4
   Interest rate .... 4%   (semiannual)
   Value from Table IV.3 .... 3.6299

   Present value of the annuity $47,189

b. Present value of the annuity:
   Payment size $13,000
   Number of payments 4
   Interest rate .... 6%   (semiannual)
   Value from Table IV.3 .... 3.4651

   Present value of the annuity $45,046

c. Present value of the annuity:
   Payment size $13,000
   Number of payments 4
   Interest rate .... 8%   (semiannual)
   Value from Table IV.3 .... 3.3121

   Present value of the annuity $43,057